DESIGNING
FOR SCREEN

DESIGNING FOR SCREEN

Production Design and Art Direction explained

Georgina Shorter

THE CROWOOD PRESS

First published in 2012 by
The Crowood Press Ltd
Ramsbury, Marlborough
Wiltshire SN8 2HR

www.crowood.com

British Library Cataloguing-in-Publication Data
A catalogue record for this book is available from the British Library.

ISBN 978 1 84797 384 9

Front cover: Top: model made by Natasha Moses; middle: illustration by Silvia
Ruiz-Poveda Lomba; bottom: stills shot from short film *Desire* (2010)
Back cover: Storyboard by Jane Morton.
Frontispiece: Aerial view of a model made by Alessandro Vitali.

Acknowledgements
I would like to thank the following people without whose help and contribution,
this book would not have been possible. Any errors are my own.
  Industry professionals: Luciana Arrighi, Eve Stewart, Jane Morton, Simon
Bowles, Tim Browning, Samantha Morton, Nicola van Gelder, Momentum
Pictures, Clare Nicholson of Company Pictures, Paul Bradley of Merchant Ivory
Productions, Paula Mackersey of McCann London (Nescafe), Drew Pautz, Phil Fisk,
Leon Westnedge; Justin Salinger, Liz White, Denise Gough, Sarah Jane Prentice,
Barbara Blyth.
  *The Art Direction for Film students at Central Saint Martins College of Art and
Design:* Fernanda Salloum, Marielle Misson Pereira, Silvia Ruiz-Poveda Lomba, Rini
Handayani, Cecily Duckett, Leighton Johns, Alessandro Vitali, Natasha Moses.
  Very special thanks to my family and friends for their contribution and support,
especially my husband Nick McCarthy, father Crispin Shorter and sisters Jacqueline
and Ana; my friends Merle Hensel, Jane Trowell and Gary Thorne.
  For the photographs, my thanks to Nick McCarthy for Figures 4–13, 77–85,
99–147.

Typeset by Jean Cussons Typsetting, Diss, Norfolk
Printed and bound in China by Everbest Printing Co. Ltd.

Contents

Introduction

A PASSION FOR FILM

I was introduced to the media of film and television at a very young age and have remained transfixed for more than thirty years. Many times, my parents despaired of my interest in anything other than escaping into a fantasy world. My mother and father, themselves, liked watching television, but enjoyed film more.

Going to the cinema was a big deal in our household. The getting ready, travelling there, then the anticipation as you entered the cinema, sitting down with some popcorn – or in those days in Singapore, sugared peanuts stuffed into a cone made from newspaper – then the excitement of the film, no matter how dire and the fun of discussing it on the way home.

The critical eye didn't come until my teens when I watched films I had liked as a child, only to discover they weren't as good as I remembered! But they were memories, and, as such, made up my childhood. It was only later that I realized that all these memories were going to become very influential in my future career choices.

Up to, and on, entering Central Saint Martins College, my focus had been on becoming a costume designer, without much thought of the set as an integral part of telling a story. However,

this rapidly changed over the course of my degree as I learned the importance of the overall visual context in helping to convey and support the cast and narrative; the idea that you could use images, colour, texture, darkness and light to captivate an audience.

This book will explore ways of designing using various media. It will look at production design for film, television and video collectively, as screen design. It will also discover the designer in you. How do you extract design information from a script? What are the key themes and how do you turn them into a concept that will support the telling of the story? Where do you begin researching and how?

The most important thing to remember – and the basis for this book – is that design is crucial to storytelling. There will be many references to existing examples of film and television, so as you read you can watch them and see and feel for yourself how their design decisions contributed to the story, making it a fuller, richer and more rounded experience for the viewer.

THE MEDIUM OF FILMING FOR SCREEN: COMPARABLE AND FUNDAMENTAL DIFFERENCES

WHAT IS ART DIRECTION?
Art direction is the term used in the film, television, commercial and music promo industries for set design. It encompasses the concept, design,

OPPOSITE: **Fig. 1   Preliminary visual for an opera made for television.**

creation and arrangement of all visual elements in a screen narrative and ensures that all conceptual ideas run consistently and coherently throughout the story. In short, it is the thread that links all visual components of the project together.

WHAT DO A PRODUCTION DESIGNER AND AN ART DIRECTOR DO?

When you sit through the credits of a film or a television show, you may be forgiven for confusing the roles of the Production Designer and the Art Director. Historically, the roles in the Art Department have been hard to define, mainly because of the ever-evolving nature of the job, the continuous changes in filmmaking techniques and the arrival of new media, such as television and computers.

The title of Art Director came about in the 1930s, when filmmaking was brought indoors thanks to artificial lighting. Before that, the closest-related credited roles were Technical Director and Interior Decorator when most shooting still took place outside. The Hollywood studio system further defined the role of art director by splitting duties between a supervising art director, who came up with the concepts, and a unit art director, who turned them into reality with a team of draughtsmen and illustrators. However, this too changed with the Supervisory Art Director becoming more of a manager – assigning a script to the Unit Art Director, who, after consultation with the Director, would come up with the designs. But, the credit would always go to the Supervisory Art Director, who had the final say, whether or not they had actually contributed.

With this fight over credit and the close working relationship developing between Art Director and Director, it became necessary to accord the position of Art Director greater status, and so the title of Production Designer came into being. First created by David O. Selznick for William Cameron Menzies in recognition of his work on *Gone With*

The Wind (1939), the new title conveyed not just the designing aspects of the job, but the collaborative nature of the role from the start of a project. Thus Art Directors became known as Production Designers and their assistants became Art Directors. (*Production Design: Architects of the Screen*, Jane Barnwell, 2004)

And they haven't changed much since. So here are the roles as they are today, though bear in mind that these distinctions are fluid.

The Production Designer, as the title indicates, is responsible for the look of the entire production. He or she, in collaboration with the Director and the Director of Photography (DoP), comes up with all the concepts and designs and oversees their execution, making sure all sets are built on time and within budget.

The Production Designer is also involved in choosing locations outside the studio and is then responsible for adapting them for the story. Generally from an artistic background, Production Designers are familiar with all technical aspects of filmmaking from camera equipment to lighting and special effects and need to be able to work within a budget. Given the vast changes in the world of filmmaking, it is essential for Production Designers to move with the times and keep up-to-date with all new design and special effects techniques.

The Art Director reports to the Production Designer and works with them to realize their vision.

Whether you have both depends on the size of the production. The more budget or the greater the size and complexity of a project, can even mean that there are several Art Directors all reporting to one Production Designer, while smaller projects only require (or can only afford one) who fulfils both roles. So, next time you watch a film or television programme, look at the credits to see which roles are listed and note that for every crew unit listed: 'first unit', 'second unit' and so on, each has its own Art Director. (*The Complete Film Dictionary,* Second Edition, Ira Konigsberg, 1997)

HOW TO USE THIS BOOK

Throughout this book, when talking about creative decision-making, I sometimes refer to Production Designers as Screen Designers. The book is, first and foremost, a tool to furnish the reader with a basic skillset with which to enter the film and television programme-making industry. It also aims to enhance the reader's design skills and techniques and to guide and encourage anyone who wants to follow a career in the industry.

1 Colour and Texture

COLOUR

For a Production Designer, colour is a vital part of communicating the visual language of a story to an audience. This chapter aims to help you start thinking about colour and texture in a different way, and to make you realize how the right emotional connection can have a profound affect on the audience.

Colour is a massive part of our everyday lives. It allows us to process, understand and relate to everything that we come into contact with, and can directly and indirectly affect our mood. Its versatility means that colour can be used in simple and complex ways to manipulate and control how we experience emotions and memories. It is a screen designer's primary tool for creating a visual language for the narrative. By providing information to the audience in this way, the Designer can convey a great deal of detail and information.

So powerful is this medium that it requires the Designer to approach a production's colour palette with considerable care and thought. Each project has its unique narrative, and you must carefully consider the colours to support and enhance that narrative. Colour should not be chosen just because you like it, but rather on the basis of how it will affect the audience.

The use of colour must come out of a complete understanding of the story and how it is told. Colour can provide a real or unreal look, depending on the form of storytelling. For example, music videos are a form of musical storytelling, where colour can be used to punctuate the melody, rhythm, narrative and mood of a song in a short space of time. Dramatic colour and unreal colour changes can grab attention and provide a more immediate experience.

This differs greatly to how colour is used in film, television, and video, where time is taken to tell the story. So, the colour palettes can be subtler, mimicking a sense of reality and authenticity. Dramatic colour changes in drama enhance the action and the narrative, for example, dream sequences that use unreal colours to indicate to the audience that this isn't reality. It can also be used as a subtle change to blur the boundaries of the real and the unreal.

Colour is especially important for lower budget productions, as it is virtually impossible to build elaborate sets without a decent budget. Through experimentation, colour can be an invaluable and effective way to communicate ideas. But before we continue discussing colour further, in terms of creating mood and atmosphere, we must understand the theory and psychology behind colour.

COLOUR THEORY

OPPOSITE: Fig. 2 **Colour and texture detail.**

Colour is the visual characteristic of refracted white

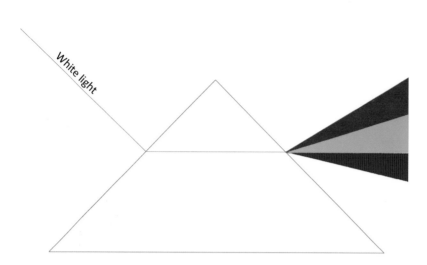

Fig. 3   How white light creates a colour spectrum when shone through a prism.

White light

light. Fig. 3 shows what happens when white light passes through a glass prism – it creates a spectrum of colour. Our eyes are only responsive to three parts of the spectrum: red, blue and green, known as the primary colours of light. When these coloured lights are blended together in different combinations, they form every single colour of light that we see.

Colour is divided into two groups: light and pigment. A lighting designer works with coloured light. The Production Designer and Art Director deal with colour in pigment form. Even though light is not a Screen Designer's medium, they must be familiar with it and the way in which it affects pigment colours.

LIGHT

Different-coloured lights can be used to produce what is known as 'additive' colour. Red, blue and green are the three elements of the spectrum that the human eye can detect and respond to. These are the basic primary additive colours for direct light, television, computer monitors, stage and screen lighting. When these colours overlap equally (Fig. 4), they create secondary colours: yellow, magenta and cyan. When all three are posi-

tioned on top of each other, they produce white light.

PIGMENT

Pigment is a substance that can change colour in reflected light by absorbing different parts of the wavelengths of that light. It is used to create paints, inks, and other materials.

Pigment has been in use for millennia and developed alongside painting. Early pigments were made from mineral or biological matter and experimented with through painting. The most vibrant pigments were purple and blue. The earliest purple pigment came from a rare species of snail, while the blue pigment was made from powdered lapis lazuli (a semi-precious stone). These striking pigments were rare and expensive, making them a symbol of wealth and power. One of the great Flemish painters, Jan Van Eyck, charged extra if clients requested those pigments in their portraits. (*Blue: The History of a Color*, Michel Pastoureau). Today, most if not all, natural and biological pigments have been replaced by synthetic ones that are less toxic, easier to use and cheaper to produce.

Primary pigment colours are different from

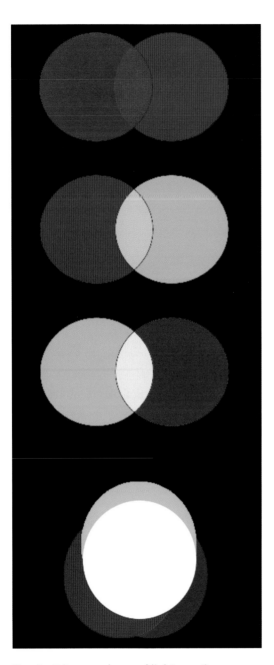

Fig. 4   Primary colours of light creating secondary colours, and white light.

Fig. 5   Primary pigment colours, when mixed in equal parts, produce the secondary colour palette.

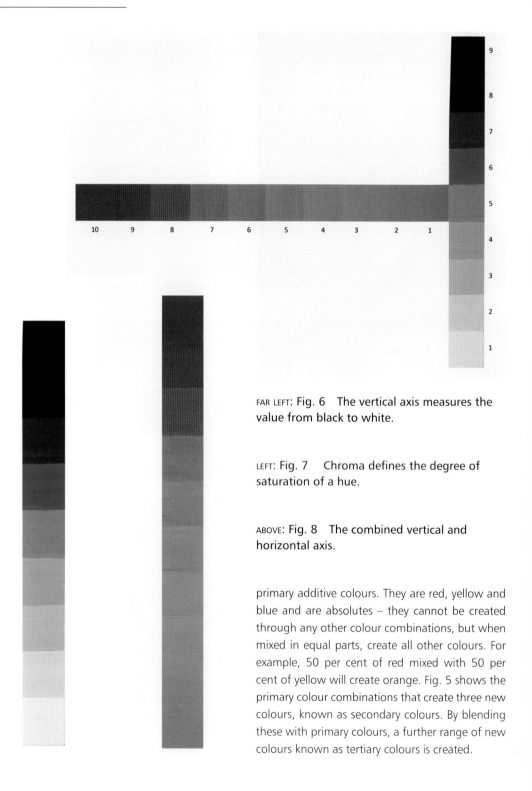

FAR LEFT: **Fig. 6**   The vertical axis measures the value from black to white.

LEFT: **Fig. 7**   Chroma defines the degree of saturation of a hue.

ABOVE: **Fig. 8**   The combined vertical and horizontal axis.

primary additive colours. They are red, yellow and blue and are absolutes – they cannot be created through any other colour combinations, but when mixed in equal parts, create all other colours. For example, 50 per cent of red mixed with 50 per cent of yellow will create orange. Fig. 5 shows the primary colour combinations that create three new colours, known as secondary colours. By blending these with primary colours, a further range of new colours known as tertiary colours is created.

THE MUNSELL COLOUR SYSTEM

Artist, teacher and inventor, Albert Munsell found a way to explain and teach the theory of colour. He developed a system that made it possible to define the hue (colour) through **value** and **chroma**. The **value** refers to the light or darkness of the **hue**, and the **chroma** is defined by its saturation and intensity. His theory is widely accepted around the world and has been used as the basis of many other systems.

HUE, VALUE AND CHROMA

Hue: distinguishes one colour from another – yellow from blue or green from red for example. It only defines each colour by name, not by lightness, darkness, strength or quality.

Value: the second dimension that tells you how light or dark a colour or hue is. Munsell created a vertical axis to measure the progression from black to white (Fig. 6).

Chroma: the third dimension that defines the strength of a colour. Chroma defines the purity of a colour in relation to grey. Colour chroma and colour saturation do not mean the same thing. Colour saturation defines its degree of purity (Fig. 7). The strength or weakness of a colour is measured on a horizontal axis. The closer to the vertical value axis, the weaker or greyer the chroma (Fig. 8). The further away from the vertical axis, the stronger and purer the hue (Fig. 9).

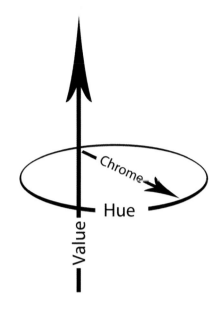

Fig. 9   Albert Munsell's colour theory.

SOME USEFUL COLOUR TERMS

- **Tint:** created by adding white to a hue.
- **Shade:** created by adding black to a hue.

Tint

Shade

Fig. 10   The difference between a tint and a shade.

- **Tone:** created by adding grey to a hue.
- **Monochrome range:** consists of shades and tints that come from the same hue.
- **Complementary hues:** colours that sit opposite each other on a colour wheel that evoke excitement.
- **Analogous hues:** are neighbouring colours that can create both harmony and disharmony.

Coloured objects in a black space appear brighter, whereas the same colour can seem darker in a white space. Higher saturated colour like red and yellow give the illusion of closer proximity to the camera because of their intensity compared to colours with lower saturation and value that give the illusion of distance.

Task 1: Create a Colour Wheel Observing Munsell's Colour Theory

1. Begin drawing a circle with a compass on a piece of white board or thick cartridge paper.
2. For this colour wheel, we will use the primary, secondary and tertiary colour range. Using a protractor, divide the circle into twelve equal parts (30°). Connect the edges of each pie shape with a straight line (Fig. 11).
3. Number each pie section from the twelve o'clock position clockwise.
4. Now assign each pie section with a colour in the following order:
   1 RED
   2 RED ORANGE
   3 YELLOW ORANGE
   4 YELLOW
   5 YELLOW GREEN
   6 GREEN
   7 BLUE GREEN
   8 GREEN BLUE
   9 BLUE
   10 VIOLET
   11 PURPLE
   12 RED PURPLE
5. Select your primary coloured paints: red, yellow and blue.
6. Use a paint medium that mixes freely with water. Gouache is used in the examples shown here. Paint the three sections in undiluted colour. Use a flat brush, keep within the lines and apply

Fig. 11   The outline of the colour wheel.

Fig. 12 Use magic tape to paint with precision.

Fig. 13 The colour wheel, complete with primary, secondary and tertiary colours.

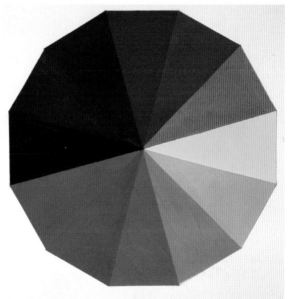

the paint evenly. Or, if you find it easier, apply removable adhesive tape for accuracy.

7. Blend the secondary colours by adding equal parts of the primary colours together.

8. Follow the same method to create the tertiary colours, using the secondary colours.

9. Make sure that the paint is dry to the touch before removing the tape. Take care to peel each strip off without taking the paint with it.

Task 2: Experiment with Value and Chroma

Value

Create a vertical axis of value from black to white in nine steps. Begin with black and white paint, and gradually mix them together to create values of grey that progress from black to white.

Chroma

Create a monochrome range. Choose a colour or hue and a grey value from the value axis. Begin with the grey value, and gradually add strength to the chosen colour until it is at its most vivid – record each sample as you go.

Quality of the Captured Image

The effect of coloured light on coloured pigment needs to be extensively tested. The quality and appearance of colour varies depending on the format and medium used to capture the image. Colour is captured differently on film stock than on video or digital. For example, film stock has a high range of contrast and is able to capture high-saturated (pure) colours compared to video. Through video the same high-saturated colours lose their definition and the edges seem to blur. Digital cameras are catching up with traditional film stock cameras, and can capture film-like images.

The grain quality of film stock can make or break the visual language of a narrative. Light grain film stock captures smooth, clean and crisp-edged images; whereas heavier grained stock captures more textures with less defined lines. This look has become associated with horror and thriller dramas, where the lack of light play tricks with the mind.

Black and White

In black and white productions, the colour spectrum does not exist. Instead it works with black and white and the number of grey shades or values in between grey scale. Working in this medium can also be termed monochromatic, as it has no hue. Filming in black and white captures colour in a distinct way. Research black and white film and photography and observe the use and variety of the grey scale. Are there shades of grey that represent different colours? Can you measure their value? Can you imagine what the image would look like in colour? How do the colours translate to a black and white or grey scale value?

Task 3: Use Black and White to Good Effect

Design an image or set in colour and then photograph it in black and white. Using Munsell's colour theory, match the values of the colours to the grey value scale. Now translate the same set into black and white, and photograph it in colour. Were your values correct? If not, repeat the experiment until you can recreate the identical values. You will find that the strength of your colours might be brash and loud in a coloured format, but when filmed in black and white the values will be similar to each other. For example, light pink and yellow can appear to have the same value in grey scale.

USING A COLOUR PALETTE TO TELL A STORY

Colour palettes are specifically created by the Production Designer, with collaboration from the Director and Director of Photography (DoP) to define a story. Using colour to complement or add contrast can greatly influence the narrative. It is an emotional element that can add symbolism, convey a mood, and add psychological impact to bring the story to life. It should unconsciously act separately from the narrative, yet work in the same rhythm. For example, colour states can change the emotion of a story and can complement the action, providing visual support during pivotal changes to move the story forward. This can set the tone and language for the whole production making it vital that all departments have a complete understanding and faith in the decisions made by the 'Creative Three' for the overall look of the piece. This in turn will determine how each scene is shot, what type of lighting should be used, what sort of film stock and camera type should be selected to achieve the look. Postproduction teams must also be kept informed to maintain and enhance the look. Extensive film stock tests need to be carried out during preproduction to ensure that the colours and overall quality of the images are being captured in the right way.

COLOUR ASSOCIATION

COLOUR AND THE SENSES

When we think of colours, we associate them with certain objects because of our culture and upbringing. As children we discover how to identify colours by association, such as, red as an apple, green as grass, yellow as the sun, blue as the sky and so on. As we move into adulthood, these associations take on deeper meanings, where we respond to colour through an emotional connection; how we feel, and how it makes us feel, not just by object association.

Observe when reading a descriptive piece of writing how colour is used to describe an environment, a situation with feeling and emotion. These associations connect with the senses (sight, smell, sound, touch, taste) creating and all-encompassing emotional experience. Think about which colours we consider loud. The brighter and more vivid the colours, the more attention-grabbing they seem. Music videos, for example, create visually interesting images to enhance the sound. Look at the colour choices and combinations. Is there a relationship between the colour and the changes in colour or are they moving in the rhythm of the music?

Consider how colour is used for specific age groups. Cartoons and children's programmes, for example, use bright, vibrant colours that young children recognize and respond to. But as children mature, the colours they see and respond to change. Bright colours become subtler, have more depth and become intellectually more stimulating. Observe the different applications of colour of a cartoon for young children and an animation for adults. Essentially, they are the same medium, but what are the differences? Which colours are used? How are the colours used to tell each story? Does the subject matter affect the way you react to the colours?

We have already looked at the physical structure of colour, but how does it affect us psychologically? Even though how a person perceives colour depends on how they mentally process it and their cultural upbringing, there are still universally accepted associations with particular groups of colours.

- **Warm colours** – red, yellow, orange. These colours evoke positive feelings of warmth, passion, happiness, and energy, but can also signify anger, hatred, aggression, and violence.
- **Cool colours** – blue, green, purple. These colours convey serenity and calmness, but also apathy, melancholy and sadness.
- **Black** – absorbs all the colours in the spectrum and can symbolize evil, death, threat, as well as power and style.
- **White** – reflects all colours in the spectrum. The opposite of black, it can symbolize youth, purity, innocence and goodness, but can also suggest sterility, and coldness.

Look at the colour red. As children, red is a strong playful colour. We relate it to apples, fire engines, London buses or post boxes (in the UK). But as adults, red can mean different associations – passion, sexuality, speed, power, strength, anger, love and, ironically, war. Think about how red is used in your daily life. Where do you see it, and how does it make you feel? Now take a look at the red on your colour wheel. Could the colour stir up one emotion more than another? How would your feelings change if we were to add black to create a darker shade of red, something that might resemble red wine? Notice how the saturation (its pureness) has disappeared, creating a much more specific colour. Recalling what red symbolizes, ask yourself what this new colour signifies. Can you connect it specifically? Choose another colour from the colour wheel and observe and note down whether they take on a more specific meaning for you.

You will find that like all creative interpretations, connecting colour with emotion through association can be very subjective. Therefore it is crucial to make sure that you are communicating the right feelings. Colour needs to be placed in context, especially cultural context, for it to have a specific meaning, and, as discussed, all colours have multiple meanings. Change the context and you could evoke a feeling opposite to that normally associated with that colour.

The importance of colour in context is evident in the world around us. Through our senses, we can be transported back in time or propelled into the future, where different combinations of colours connect to memories. But what helps us form memories? What influences us? Can the method in which the image is captured really influence how we imagine a period in time to be? Like an art historian, a Production Designer will carry out detailed visual research (photography, books, drawings, film/video, paintings) to build up a mental picture of life in another time. How these colours looked back then and how they look to us today depended on the 'technology' available at the time and can ultimately influence what colour palette a designer will use to capture the essence of it.

CULTURAL INTERPRETATIONS

Around the world, people from different cultures view colours in different ways. This is a hugely important consideration for a Production Designer, as the symbolic value of that colour will have an emotional affect on the viewer. For example, in Western cultures, a bride wears white on her wedding day, whereas in China or India she wears red. Using the list below, research the emotional connection of the colours, and how they are perceived in the major cultures of the world.

- Red
- Blue
- Green
- Purple
- Yellow
- Orange
- Pink
- White
- Black

The following dramas show how a very specific colour palette can define an era, helping to tell a story.

MAD MEN (2007 – PRESENT)

Set in the late 1950s on the east coast of America, this television series follows the professional and private lives of the employers and employees of a successful advertising agency during the social, political and economical climate of that time. Using a restrained and sophisticated colour palette, such as deep rich colours against a backdrop of warm neutral colours helps to differentiate the masculine advertising world of the city from the homely world of the suburbs, where the focus is on family values and traditional gender roles. As the series progresses, the characters in this world move into the 1960s, and have to adapt to its changes. The design team takes this into consideration by transforming the warm sophisticated colours of the ideal-oriented 50s into the bright intense hues of the swinging 60s.

ASHES TO ASHES (2008)

The colour palette sets the scene in this BBC television drama, where DI Alex Drake is shot in 'our' present, and wakes up in 1981, where she leads a parallel life as a police detective whilst lying in a coma back in 'our' time. Colour is used to differentiate between the two lives. Her comatose state has a cold palette, featuring varying grey values and grey blues that stir up feelings of coldness, sterility, and lifelessness. This is in sharp contrast to her parallel existence in 1980s London with its vibrant, brash colours and striking combinations, symbolic of the period's cultural revolution and social upheaval.

HERO (2002)

This film presents four different interpretations in a very stylised way. The role of colour is simplistic and extremely effective in differentiating between each version of the events (red, green, blue and white), as well as helping to boost the story's emotion and mood. By using blocks of vivid colour and a variety of textural elements, a beautiful ethereal contrast is added to soften scenes that would otherwise be dominated by the striking Chinese architecture. Flowing, layered materials are used both in set and costume to help accentuate the skill and agility of the characters, and their respective emotional states beneath the guise of feared assassins.

Hero is set in China during the Warring States period (approximately 227BCE), when all states were rebelling against unification. It tells the epic story of a nameless prefect from a small area in the Qin state, who travels to the capital city for an audience with the king, who has survived three attempts on his life by three notorious assassins (Long Sky, Broken Sword and Flying Snow). To protect himself from further attempts, he stops visitors coming within 100 paces of his person. When Nameless arrives, he proudly announces that he has killed the king's most feared assassins and is invited to come closer and recount his tales of heroism. The king does not believe his tales and offers his own interpretation of events as he has personally experienced the strength and skill of these assassins. The Director Zhang Yimou, along with Production Designers Tingxiao Huo and Zhenzhou Yi, created a production full of vibrant colour and strong visuals. They were very successful in using the psychology of colour to tell the narrative. It is the heart of this story and Zhang Yimou believes that because of this the film will stay in people's memories.

…a few years later, if someone mentions Hero, you are going to remember the colours. You are going to remember in a sea of golden leaves, two ladies dressed in red are dancing in the air. You are going to remember, on a lake as still as a mirror, two men are using their swords to convey their sorrow like birds flying on the water like dragonflies. It is images like these that will leave lasting impressions in the minds of the audience.

(Zhang Yimou, interviewed for 'Hero' Defined: A look at the epic masterpiece, by Elite Group Enterprises, 2004)

SLEEPY HOLLOW (1999)

This is the story of Constable Ichabod Crane who is sent from New York City to investigate a series of murders in a remote Dutch farming community, where everyone lives in fear of the Headless Horseman. Ichabod, who comes from a world of science and reason, has his world turned upside down when he is thrust into another full of myth, magic, witchcraft and superstition. The genre of the film is horror and the lack of colour, muted hues and use of black, white and grey scale work well with the subdued light to create an eerie ambience. This contrasts greatly with the use of strong vivid colours of red and white in Ichabod's dream sequences as a child. Director Tim Burton and Production Designer Rick Heinrichs created a dark period fairytale-like horror inspired by the gothic Hammer Horror films of the 1950s through to the 1970s (TimeOut Film Guide 2011). The dramatic colour palette used was integral to the telling of this story. The use of black and shades of blue blacks, greys of varying value and muted colours give the film the impression of being in black and white, helping to create the feeling of a town in the grip of a nightmare. Controlling the light and using shadows helped to enhance the atmosphere with horrific authenticity. Also, the use of monochrome colours, black, charcoals, greys and muted colours helped to differentiate wealth and status in the small town compared to the utilitarian, ordered colours of the city.

In the following two examples of film based on the lives of artists, the Production Designer used the style of the painter's work to compose painterly-like visuals.

FRIDA (2002)

Colour is used to great effect in this film, where it represents and illustrates the painter Frida Kahlo's life and work. The palette of high saturated colours helps to capture the essence of the Mexican culture, of which she was tremendously proud. The brightness also helps capture the tumultuous life she led due to her serious physical injuries that left her barren and plagued her till her death, and the all-consuming love she had for her philandering husband, mural artist Diego Rivera. This production is a good example of how the colour palette used in her paintings was continued throughout the film design, connecting art to life and back to art again.

GIRL WITH THE PEARL EARRING (2003)

Set in Delft, Holland, in 1665, it tells the story of a peasant girl, who becomes the assistant and eventual muse for the painter Vermeer. The quality and the colours of the palette mirror the essence of Vermeer's paintings. These visual choices help to define the story's place in history, setting the action in a believable time. Like Julie Taymor's Frida, this production uses a similar formula to translate the story from canvas to film.

TEXTURE

Texture is the surface quality of any substance. Texture allows us to differentiate between different tactile experiences like smooth and rough, sheen and dull, fur or weave, stone or metal, etc. and connects them with our senses to evoke feelings. Very much like colour, texture can trigger a memory.

This element works hand in hand with colour, as it gives authenticity to a story. Like colour, it adds another feature to the appearance of objects and matter, and gives the story a tactile dimension. It can also illustrate a period in time, a place and the passing of time. It can also show poverty or wealth. A Designer has to be sensitive to all of this. For instance, to create a believable old and dilapidated apartment, a Designer would either need old materials and furnishings, or new furnishings that have been 'treated' to look old. A lot depends on how the story is being told, and a Designer must pay close attention to that.

VERA DRAKE (2004)

The story is set in London after World War II in the 1950s, a time when everyone had experienced some level of personal loss. Vera Drake, a bubbly wife and mother, who is portrayed as a saint, looks after her family, cleans palatial houses of the wealthy, and helps out girls 'in trouble' by performing illegal abortions. Her family, unaware of her double life, is shocked at the revelation when one of the girls she helps dies of complications. The bleakness of working class London is captured through the subdued lighting, dark colour palette and texture of a world still gripped by the after-effects of war. The use of dark heavy colours such as greys, dark blues, greens and browns reflects a society burying secrets rather than openly discussing them. These colours used for Vera Drake's tiny, cramped but

Fig. 14   How colour and texture can create authenticity.

Fig. 15   Colour and texture creating authenticity.

warm front room/dining room contrast strongly with the brighter spaces and light coloured walls and carpets of the palatial home she cleans, and later the prison cell she is confined to where the harshness of the grey white tiles helps to convey feelings of isolation, loneliness and despair.

Texture can trick the viewer into thinking a colour is more intense and saturated than it actually is. Consider the saturation quality of two cubes. Both cubes are the same size, hue, value and chroma. However, one of the cubes has a semi gloss surface, while the other is matte. Observe whether the colours look the same. Does one cube have a more intense colour than the other? Notice how the cube with the high gloss sheen creates a much more intense colour than the matte surface. Smooth surfaces trick the mind into thinking that the colour is of a higher saturation when in fact it is exactly the same. The same would be true if you used the same colour of paint, but one was gouache and the other acrylic (Fig. 16); the acrylic paint would come across as having a higher intensity.

In production, there is a need to use materials that are practical and easy to come by. The majority of sets on sound stages are build of wood, but by using different techniques, materials and finishes, the wooden walls can be transformed into eighteenth century French mahogany for example. Specialist painters in art departments have the expertise to transform this basic material into anything. The next time you watch a drama on the big screen or in the comfort of your living room, see if you can tell the difference between genuine and mock materials.

COLOUR AND TEXTURE

Design, as we know, is very subjective. Memories are influenced by many elements that explain why my interpretation of a situation will differ from someone else's. However, the use of a colour or texture can immediately trigger something within the audience, helping to engage them, and this is what the Production Designer aims to achieve – an emotional connection with the audience.

Fig. 16 The same paint applied to different surfaces can create varying levels of intensity.

Task 4: Build Your Own Set

With all that has been discussed in this chapter, experiment with creating the following moods:
Happy
Sad
Sinister
Exciting
Decide on a mood and create a set using colour and texture, and record it on camera (digital, film or video). Now change the colour and texture to convey another mood, again capturing the image in the same way. Continue doing this for the next two moods. Now consider the differences between the sets. How do they differ? Review the rushes to see how you did. Did the captured images match your intentions? Show these images to someone else to see if they pick up the same feelings.

2 Creating an Environment

OBJECTS IN SPACE

Previously, we introduced the importance of colour and texture, and how they can create feelings, emotions and mood through psychology and association. This chapter aims to bring those design elements further into context by linking them with space to see how they help create and define an environment.

Space can be defined as a free area that can have a specific purpose; site specific. We can also say that a space is ambiguous until objects and other design elements are placed in it to give it meaning. For example, an empty room with bare walls can be transformed into a very specific space by applying particular colours and textures. In much the same way a blank canvas can have a multitude of meanings until colour, texture and form are applied, when it is transformed into something very specific.

Imagine an empty room with a white floor and smooth walls painted with white emulsion paint. Ask yourself: how has the matte white paint transformed the room? How do you feel about it? Is it still a blank canvas or is it stirring up other feelings? Remember what was discussed in the previous chapter about white and answer the following questions: Does the room have a warmth about

OPPOSITE: **Fig. 17   Location research of Sicilian churches.**

it? Does the white amplify its emptiness? What feelings does it evoke? Purity and innocence are associated with white but can they be associated with this space? Probably not – however, without definition of texture and shade the space can feel empty and unfeeling – even sterile.

Now imagine if we introduce a texture into the space, for example large, white thick-pile rug that covers a third of the floor space. Observe the effect that this new textural addition has made to the space. From a space that exhibited coldness and emptiness, it is transformed into a space that has a softer, playful and comfortable side. Now remove the rug and introduce white ceramic tiles on all four walls and the floor. What has happened to the space now? Notice how the room's colour has stayed exactly the same, yet the textural material has given the room a whole new meaning and purpose.

Observe the transition from a room that evoked feelings of comfort and softness, it has been transformed into quite the opposite. The smooth, hard surface of the tiles transports us into a colder environment. This is because we associate different feelings with different textural objects. We know that a fluffy rug is going to feel soft and inviting, while ceramic tiles are going to feel cold and hard... making the space seem uncomfortable and clinical. The field has been narrowed down but there is still room to be more specific as the space is still largely undefined. Why is the ambiguity still apparent, especially as we have attempted to define the texture and colour? Experiment with the following task.

Task 1: Transform a White Space

Transform the same space into the following, using one block colour and a block texture (no patterns or prints) to define them.

- Kitchen
- Bathroom
- Doctor's surgery

Observe your choices. Were you successful in changing the spaces in each instance? Test it out on a friend. Present the three environments to them and without hinting, ask them to identify the purpose of each space. Did they give you the right answer straight away, or did they give several answers or pose further questions? The latter is most likely to be correct because colour and texture alone cannot specify a space. When introducing paint and pattern to colour and texture, they begin to take on much more detail, helping to create a purposeful environment. Using certain types of print or pattern can create an historical or contemporary setting. Using a heavy, deep-coloured, velvet flock wallpaper, for example, can suggest a time of richness and decadence – more akin to a period setting than a contemporary one. However, you should pay careful attention when selecting patterns, as some may look too contemporary on their own.

Introducing a variety of colours and shades helps to create life. Every object that we look at is made up of more than a single colour. Observe an object that is apparently of single colour. You will be able to detect that even though the object is all one colour, it has shades and tints that give it a 3-D quality. This is achieved through the use of light – observe how light hits the object. Can you determine the direction from which the light comes? Understanding how objects appear in light is an essential part of a Designer's job.

However, when objects are introduced to a space it immediately it becomes specific and gains a context. When light is shone on an object, one colour appears to have several colours. The sides that are further away from the light appear darker than the sides lit by the light. This helps to define form and surface. Observe an object in light, and note how light affects it. Notice the colour and shades, and how it defines the form and surface area.

When you bring the combination of colour and texture into a third dimension, you need to create depth of field. Using a single colour and texture, the space remains flat and artificial, even though it is a living space. Combining helps bring life to a space, transforming it into a more believable space. Using a variety of colours and textures adds depth and dimension through layering.

Patterns and prints add another layer of dimension to the space. Each pattern and print can enhance a colour or texture, bringing them to life, or combined in a harmonious arrangement to add much needed depth and definition. In Peter Greenaway's film, *The Cook, the Thief, his Wife and her Lover* (1989), extensive colour schemes and flamboyant prints were not needed to create impact. Instead, each scene has a carefully chosen colour palette that represents a theme, as the production's Designer Ben van Os explains:

Red in the restaurant to evoke decadence; blue in the exterior set suggested the city; green in the kitchen represented what was new and organic and growing; white in the toilets symbolized purity and innocence; yellow characterized the Lover's antique books.

(Ettedgui, 1999, pg. 159)

Even though he was limited to selected colours, Ben van Os successfully created tremendous depth in each scene, by combining the colours with different textured materials and objects. The restaurant scenes were played out in grand surroundings, using heavy fabrics, such as brocades and velvets, with gold trimmings. He created blocks of colour for each scene, but it was the variety of textural fabrics and objects that he chose that created such a powerful impact. His use of regal materials, such as velvets, brocades, satins, silks and patterned wallpapers helped to create a scene full of decadence and opulence.

In contrast, the kitchen was a place where the cook's culinary masterpieces were born, and the place where Georgina and Michael conduct their love affair under the nose of her husband. Untainted love and nutritional food were nurtured under the protection of the cook.

Another important factor in how we see colour and texture on screen, is how light affects them. Without light there is to way no define them. Light helps bring out depth and intensity. It is a powerful thing that can enhance, or conversely bleach out colour and textural character, and it must never be ignored. Designer Ben van Os was very influenced by the production's Director of Photography, Sacha Vierny.

I always paid a great deal of attention to where the light came from when I worked as an interior designer and light has become even more important to me in film....

His [Sacha Vierny] cinematography is very painterly; he lights in layers, giving the image great depth and richness.

(Ettedgui, 1999, pg 159)

Ben van Os' thoughts emphasize the need for Designers to be aware of light sources, and of the importance of the relationship between Designer and DoP.

CONTEXT

Creating context is a vital part of the design process. Earlier we identified how colours, textures and objects need to work together to create a contextual backdrop for the narrative to begin. Context is not only about creating beautiful settings, but more importantly, creating environments that tell a story.

Composition means arranging objects in space and is central to creating an environment. You can learn much about composition from the creative discipline of interior design. It takes into account any source of light, the room's character and history and the personalities of the inhabitants; all of which are significant factors for a screen designer. Of course, unlike interior designers, we are not always creating idyllic environments, but it is still worth learning from its rules on arrangement and composition.

Look at any interior design magazine and see how furniture is arranged in a space (pay attention to layouts in interior and architectural magazines). Notice how colour and texture are applied for impact, and how the combination creates ambience in a room. Interior design adopts tricks/ design rules that can help make the most of the space that you have at your disposal. For example, certain groups of colours can complement a space and others can distort it.

Light colours have an expanding effect, while darker colours do the opposite, causing a constricting effect. Presented with a small space, interior designers choose lighter colours to give the illusion of space. The same effect can be achieved if light colours are applied to a large space. Think of specific places where this technique is adopted. In this case, the light colours reflect, creating a space that seems even larger – thus distorting it. Consider the colour of the ceiling – white adds height to a room, where as a darker colour shortens it.

Conversely, applying darker colours to a small space, contracts and creates the illusion that it is smaller than it actually is. Dark colours in larger rooms make the rooms look smaller. It's not uncommon for stately homes to use darker colours and heavier fabrics in large spaces – they add grandeur to an already large space. Heavier fabrics were also functional – they kept the draft out and the warmth in.

Another essential interior design principle for screen design is the size and scale of objects, prints, patterns and furniture. For an interior designer, these environments need to create a harmonious effect, as they will either be used as living or workspaces. So, choosing oversized prints in a small room with little light, for example, would never be recommended. Similarly, placing a large three-piece sofa into a pokey living room, or a small sofa in a large loft space would not be ideal. The focus on style and design is integral to achieving a harmonious and convivial effect.

These principles are also important for a Screen Designer but for very different reasons. The production design must support the narrative; therefore harmonious spaces are only used if it serves the story; the ability to control and even distort a space is crucial. By applying distortion you are making a comment on the environment and giving it meaning. A viewer can make very quick observations about a space. For example, if an elaborate three-piece suite is crammed into a very small front room, what are you saying about this space and the people who live in it? Have the owners lost

everything and been forced to downsize? Is the furniture a reminder of a past life of riches? Or do they live beyond their means afraid to lose face?

The type and style of furniture is essential too. Specific styles and designs, and whether new, old, or in a state of decay, give meaning to the space. Vertical stripes and patterns add height to a room. Painting the ceiling a lighter colour also gives a room height and expanse, whereas dark-coloured ceilings create a feeling of constriction and compression. The key is to understand these design conventions before you start.

Select objects for a space with care. Throwing caution to the wind or filling a space with 'stuff' does not necessarily add value to the story. Even the most cluttered sets have been carefully organized. Production Designers and Set Decorators painstakingly choose objects that will go together to reflect the concept, themes and the essence of an environment. A lot of research is done to ensure that each object has merit, and is vital for a scene. The devil is in the detail. Set dressing is hugely important, as *Upstairs Downstairs* Production Designer, Eve Stewart, explains:

> Well, we're lucky in this country that there's still a lot of it about. And I'm kind of a constant weasel of getting to different places – I go around markets and fairs and auctions. With my decorator, we managed to purchase all the stuff. We hired a few bits, like the tiger's head, but a lot of things were purchase.
>
> (Eve Stewart in an interview with Barrett Bountas in *Masterpiece*, February, 2011, www.pbs.org/wgbh/masterpiece/ upstairsdownstairs/stewart.html)

The arrangement of furniture and objects can send subtle messages to the audience. Take another look at an interior magazine and observe people's homes. How are spaces are laid out? Study what

Fig. 18   Details provide insight into how a person lives.

personal objects people have on show in those spaces. Notice that they may not be functional, but selected for aesthetic reasons. These little details add insights into a space and to a person's character.

So, the placement and the significance of the layering and type of dressing strengthen the visuals. For example, visualize a sofa. If you add a cushion, what are you telling the audience? Would the message be different if you chose a different style of cushion or would it stay the same? Consider the way these objects are positioned. Are they a reflection of the inhabitants or is it comment on the story?

Look around your own home and analyse any key objects that describe you as an individual. Do you see organization and uniformity or chaos? Are things haphazardly displayed? Is there a definite style or a mix of styles?

The personalities presented on screen are crucial to telling stories about people. Director Wes Anderson, along with his Production Designers, provided a visual history of his characters, for instance in *The Royal Tenenbaums* (2001), *The Life Aquatic with Steve Zissou* (2004) and *Fantastic Mr Fox* (2009). Working closely together, the Production Designer and Set Decorator visualize scenarios that contain a wealth of information.

ARCHITECTURE: BUILDING AN ENVIRONMENT

Understanding architecture and applying your knowledge of the theory is a huge part of being a Screen Designer. An ability to create a world where narrative and action take place is essential. Structures bring more dimension, more interest and more authenticity to a set. It feeds our imagination and draws us into a world.

Gone are golden days of Hollywood, when cityscapes were painted on backdrops to give a sense of place. In the last fifty years, designers have been captivated by the power of architecture, and how it allows boundless versatility and imagination. Production Designer, Ken Adam, who designed the early James Bond films, such as *Dr. No* (1962) and *Goldfinger* (1964), and *The Madness of King George* (1994), discusses his background with Peter Ettedgui:

> …I followed Korda's (Vincent) advice to study architecture first… this background gave me a knowledge of different period styles and made it easy for me to provide a functional acceptable set.
>
> (Ettedgui, 1999, pg 25)

Fig. 19   Architecture as a powerful form of visual language.

The benefits of featuring architecture are that it can help express a period of time, a place, a mood as well as expressing personal style and design. Architecture can bring comfort and tranquility, or, conversely, harshness and cold (*see* Figs 19 to 21). It can make us stand back in awe of its engineering brilliance – which makes it attractive to Screen Designers. The materials used, the way they are constructed, the effect of light as it ricochets off the surfaces, all affect the way we feel.

This structural design surrounds us every day – modern skyscrapers or historic palaces, are all part of our everyday lives. All these structures are constructed with materials that tell us a story of time. Creating such amazing structures on screen is only half the battle. You need to see how a building has aged and how the elements have changed it to get a more in-depth knowledge about the passing of time. Paying special attention to how materials age helps a Designer create authenticity. For example, consider how copper, shiny and brilliant when new, oxidizes into shades of green, or how stone decays when exposed to centuries of weather and pollution.

These observations are vital when reproducing structures for the screen. Each building has its own character, and tells a different story, so it is crucial

Fig. 20   Architecture as a powerful form of visual language – power and modernity.

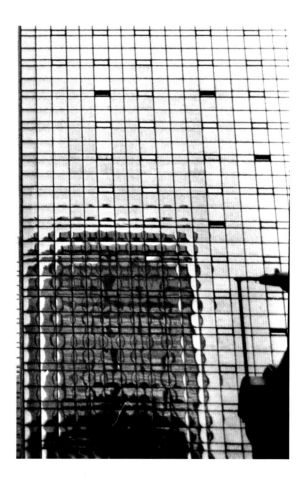

Fig. 21   Architectural surfaces can reflect and distort.

that you make the right selection. Unlike functioning buildings, a screen set has a much shorter life span. In *Sets in Motion: Art Direction and Film Narrative,* Charles Affron and Mirella Jona Affron discuss some interesting comparisons between architecture and set design by observing six principle statements by author Juan Antonio Ramírez, of *La Arquitectura en el Cine: Hollywood, la edad de oro (Architecture in cinema: Hollywood, the golden age).*

1. Film décor is fragmentary; only that which is necessary to the shooting is built or simulated through painting or miniature [meaning that whatever is fundamental to the shoot is built, or recreated in miniature or in painting. Rather than building an entire structure, you only build that which is necessary.]
2. It alters size and proportion; depending on the illusion sought, it is either bigger or smaller than the scale demanded by architectural authenticity. [Screen sets are rarely replicated on a 1:1 scaled ratio. Their purpose is to capture the authenticity rather than scale, depending on whether the desired illusion needs to be bigger or smaller.]
3. It is rarely orthogonal; it follows a logic that is not architectural. The camera, the trapezoidal constructions, slopings, and angles necessary to the desired effect do not appear as deformations. [Meaning that it is rarely perpendicular i.e. right angles.]
4. It is hyperbolic; it abolishes the insignificant and exaggerates either in the direction of simplicity or complexity.
5. It is mobile, flexible, even elastic; it can be used and reused. [The set can be used and recycled when budgets are limited.]
6. It is built rapidly and rapidly demolished;

its cost, often as great as or greater than the architecture it emulates, has value only as photograph.

(Affron, 1995, p. 31)

Architecture has a permanence – it is built to fulfil a purpose, while a filmed/recorded or photographed set has a life as long as the production process. The longevity of the recorded image is closer to the actual architecture that it represents.

The use of architecture in this medium was influenced by stage design, where structures were constructed to support a story. However, it was always restricted to the stage; a method that did not lend itself to camera work. The movement of the camera plays a huge role in storytelling. There are few times when a camera remains static, it is constantly on the move, capturing everything on screen.

Storytelling through architecture is an exciting prospect for any designer. When used correctly it has the ability to pull us back in time or propel us forward into exciting and new worlds. Architecture helps to place us in a specific time, past, present or future.

MANIPULATING SURROUNDINGS

In Jane Barnwell's book *Production Design: Architects of the Screen* (p.25 onwards), she discusses environments, and most importantly how one can manipulate a city, so that it is in tune with the story's narrative. You can do this by controlling what you show the audience and how you control the life of the city, by being selective with the areas you choose to paint the narrative's picture.

The city of London, like most cities, has many faces. It can be seen as a vibrant, affluent, creative and cutting edge, but on the flip side, it can also be a cold, unfriendly, even dangerous place, where you can quickly become a nobody. Cities like

Fig. 22   The time of day impacts on how you feel about a place.

London are easily recognisable by their skylines, and controlling the use of them, ultimately controls how you view a place.

In Michael Winterbottom's *Wonderland* (1999), the London he creates is a lonely city, with a subdued colour palette; quite a departure from the excitement and beauty that we might associate with it. *Wonderland* was shot in Soho and in southwest London with minimal crew that captured a side of suburban London that enhanced the story of a South London family with great realism.

This is the polar opposite to Roger Michell's *Notting Hill* (1999), which was made in the same year, but portrayed London in a completely different way. Where *Wonderland* focused on a family's struggles and feelings of loneliness, *Notting Hill* painted London in a much brighter, happier, more affluent light. Think about the various guises of the city of New York; like London, it is a sprawling metropolis, and yet notice how it is manipulated in *You've Got Mail* (1998) where it is a light and fluffy place, funny and colourful, compared to *Taxi Driver* (1976) or *Saturday Night Fever* (1977), which shows a much grittier seedier side.

These comparisons can be drawn against many film, television or video works – we can say that the narratives, genre and subject matter are more important and are ultimately the driving forces behind why we would depict a place in a specific way – however, the art of manipulation is a valuable skill...one that you may not know you already have.

Task 2: Recreate a Screen Version of Your Home Town

Now put this theory into practice. Try to capture the essence of your home city or town. Armed with a camera, embark on a photo walk around your town. Can you capture its soul?

Once you have completed your expedition, ask yourself these questions: When did you choose to do your walk? During the day or night or both? Where did you go? Now collate your images and then group and analyse them. What did you focus on? Did you include landmarks, famous buildings, or a familiar unmistakable skyline? Did you include your favourite parts of the city that mean something to you?

Establish what picture you have painted with your images. Now consider the way you captured the images – what type of device did you use? If you used a camera, was it digital, film, or LOMO? Did you choose colour or black and white? If you chose colour, experiment with converting the same images into black and white – what happens to the city?

Notice how the buildings change, and how the monochromatic version makes you focus on the values of black, grey and white as well as the textural quality of the surface. Notice how the quality of the image also pays a huge part in the capturing of a place.

Now see how the same location can change at different times of day – think how these simple decisions can shape the images that you capture. Ultimately, the story controls the direction that you go in to achieve the visual language.

This task will help you understand the importance of the world around you. How the Designer can capture the atmosphere, the way light falls and illuminates structures, objects, people, the importance of colour and texture, all these factors help us gain awareness on how we view the world. It is only through research, observation and understanding that we can even begin to consider what it means to replicate it. Production Designer Christopher Hobbs believes this is vital:

> I also advise anyone who wants to be a production designer to become an observer. Don't just glance at the world, really look at it, and analyse it.
>
> (Ettedgui, 1999, 131)

PERIOD, CONTEMPORARY OR FUTURE?

Screen Designers work within the confines of a specific world, no matter where it is, making it accessible to a modern audience. We are lucky that we can still see so much historical architecture today. Our skylines are littered with historical buildings and monuments that give us great insight into how people lived in centuries gone by.

It is vital that you can identify periods correctly. Today's audiences demand accuracy and authenticity when capturing the feel and spirit of the era of a story, down to the year and, in some cases, to the month, week(s) or day(s) (if re-telling historical events). Being able to include historical architectural elements can add another layer of dimension to the storytelling.

PERIOD DRAMA

There are two types of historical or period drama. The first is factually correct re-enactment of factual historical events. The other uses the period or historical events as a backdrop for a fictional story. There are also dramatizations of books, written in a contemporary time, that are now considered period to us, for example E.M. Forster's *Howards End*, *The Portrait of a Lady* by Henry James or *Jane Eyre* by Charlotte Brontë.

One question that you should ask is: how far do you go with recreating a period if money and time are no obstacle? Maybe the key question should not be how far do you go, but how far can you go, or need to go? There are two trains of thought – Designers need to avoid being too generalist when capturing a period, because one can run the risk of destabilizing the story telling. As Vincent LoBrutto says in his book *The Filmmaker's guide to Production Design*:

> Generalizing the time and place can weaken a story or disorient the nature of the narrative. New York in 1961 is not the same as New York in 1968. They are both in the 1960s, but stylistic, cultural, and political factors changed dramatically during these years.
>
> (LoBrutto, 2002, pg103)

Fig. 23 Illustration from *Howard's End* (1992) by Luciana Arrighi. Courtesy of Merchant Ivory Productions.

Fig. 24   Illustration from *Remains of the Day* (1993) by Luciana Arrighi. Courtesy of Merchant Ivory Productions.

Audiences may forgive inaccuracies in period dramas set more than 200 years ago, but they always expect to be transported into another time, so the Designer has a duty to deliver as accurate a vision as possible to serve the story.

Designers need to be able to give their audiences a silent narrative through a competent level of accuracy. Nowadays, audiences are shrewder than they have ever been, and cannot be palmed off. We no longer live in a time when screen design was in its infancy, and historical inaccuracies weren't huge issues, because audiences marvelled at this new medium of film. Now, more than 100 years on, Designers have a duty to keep that bond between artist and audience strong by creating a world that is as believable as it is exciting. Authenticity is vital, which means observing, researching and most importantly understanding the period in which the story unfolds, as Production Designer Luciana Arrighi explains:

> Once you are sure of your period, you don't have to follow it faithfully. What I don't like much is mucking about with what one doesn't understand...
>
> (Interview with author, 2011)

Choosing artistic licence over historical accuracy,

in the hope that your audience won't notice the discrepancies, means you tread a fine line.

When working with Director James Ivory, Production Designer Luciana Arrighi made sure she understood the periods she needed to depict.

> ...he [James Ivory] wanted the look to be as true to the period as possible...
>
> (Interview with author, 2011)

Figs 23 and 24 show how much historical detail she had to provide to achieve the right look and feel for each period.

Focusing on historical architecture can help, but the need to understand how people lived, their culture, what was going on politically as well as socially at the time is crucial for scene setting. There are many avenues available to help identify specifics. A lot has been documented in literature, painting, exteriors and interiors have been preserved and restored, and since the last century, photography – all offer detailed insights into other times. Being able to distinguish particular style, materials, colours, textures, design and silhouettes from one period to the next is key. You need to know your Art Deco from your Art Nouveau, for example, and be able to recognize that nineteenth-century England is different from nineteenth-century France. Both are European, but look different. The same is true of Northern America and Canada.

It is also important to determine whether your story takes place in the city or in the country, or in wealthy or poor circumstances – this is very important in historical drama as there are great differences between them. Don't forget though, that as designers you are adding your own interpretation, even if it is historically based. As Gerry Scott, Production Designer on BBC's *Pride and Prejudice* (1995) says:

> Though I like to be historically accurate as possible, I'm not prepared to be a slave to

it. It's important to understand the way people lived in 1813, but we are not making an academic study of the period; it's more important to grasp the spirit of the time. In any case, even if we had all the time and money in the world, we could never be completely accurate, because an awful lot of things we'd need no longer exist, except perhaps in museums.

> (Birtwistle and Conklin, 1995, p. 35)

ORLANDO (1992)

Sally Potter's *Orlando* is a very good example of how differences can be illustrated effectively. Based on Virginia Woolf's novel, *Orlando: A Biography*. We first meet Orlando as a young man in Elizabethan England (1600). Elizabeth I gives him land and a stately home for his children, and children's children, on the condition that he never grows old. The narrative progresses through specific moments in time relating to important emotional points in his life: 1610 – falling in love (Stuart England), 1650 – becoming a poet (Commonwealth England), 1700 – politics (Restoration England).

Orlando travels to Constantinople as the British Ambassador, where he wakes one morning to find that he his no longer a man, but a woman. On her return to England in 1750 – women and society (Georgian England), enquiries are made into whether Orlando was always a woman, resulting in the loss of his/her fortune. The narrative moves to 1850 (Victorian England), where Orlando is about to lose everything, when she meets Shelmerdine, an American traveller with whom she becomes romantically involved.

We then travel into World War II where she is heavily pregnant, into the present day (1990s), where she recounts the extraordinary adventures of her life for a publisher. The Production Designer successfully captured the spirit of each era through architecture, style, culture and detail. The Production Designer captured Orlando's world and how it changed through time and more importantly how the change in gender affected Orlando's life.

ASHES TO ASHES (2008 TO 2010)

This BBC television series is still to be considered a period drama even though it is set only in the 1980s. With the advantage of film and television footage and a surge in the technological age, the essence is captured through the design, style, culture and music of the time. The use of actual footage of London adds reality and captures the popular culture and energy of 1981, a volatile time.

Anachronisms are a challenge for any designer trying to create a foolproof image of the past, whether they are due to budget or time constraints, or any other factor. The trick is to recognize when a set becomes a study rather than encapsulating its soul. Aficionados will always scrutinize and pick up anomalies, but as discussed before, the aim is to keep them to a minimum. In *Ashes to Ashes*, Gene Hunt's Audi Quattro was apparently not available in the UK in right hand drive in 1981; however, the car was chosen because it matched the character.

CONTEMPORARY SETTINGS

In more contemporary settings, historical buildings are now our homes, museums, restaurants, sport centres, and so on, provide a visual feast for the viewer. These buildings in contemporary settings add substance, iconic buildings passing through time. Contemporary drama showcases stories that are taking place now, including what is happening politically, culturally and socially. A lot of present day structures are influenced by elements such as light (considered to be one of the most important elements), current awareness for the environment (materials used) and social consciousness.

Architects look closely at the impact any new building will have on the existing surroundings. And the same can be said about Screen Designers. We are in the business of creating different worlds, therefore it is imperative that we explore and observe what already exists, and how that impacts our lives and ultimately our creative work. A lot of new constructions have influences from the past, in particular the 1950s and 1960s – a time that many consider the birth of modern design. We have a ferocious appetite for vintage design and architecture.

Current dramas quickly become dated. For example, think about the events that can be dated after pivotal moments in time. For example think about the change of iconic skyline, such as New York City after 9/11 or in Europe, after the fall of the Berlin Wall.

In Wolfgang Becker's *Goodbye Lenin!* (2003), he captures the impact and changes that happen with the fall of the Berlin Wall, when East and West Germany unite. *Goodbye Lenin!* sets the story in 1989 East Germany during a political protest where a mother sees her son being arrested and suffers a heart attack, which puts her into a coma. Several months later she wakes up in 1990 and, unbeknownst to her, her beloved East Germany no

Task 3: Create a Current and Future Cityscape

Take your camera and observe your city again. This time look for surroundings that exhibit contemporary and futuristic qualities. What is it about the structures that you have chosen that make them contemporary or futuristic? Is it the silhouette? The materials used? Can you identify characteristics?

longer exists. However, under her doctor's strict orders, she must avoid all forms of excitement for fear of a relapse.

Her son and friends, realizing that she mustn't find out about the unification, confine her to her apartment, and go to great lengths to recreate East German life, with television, repackaging food and so on, anything to stop her realizing how much change there has been since she was in the coma. These sorts of narratives help us understand what an effect world events or events in a specific time have on our lives and designers need to recognize and pay attention to that change.

FUTURISTIC

Futuristic design was born out of relating to the past, many futuristic cities captured on screen were inspired by buildings and structures from the past. *Blade Runner* (1982), for example, creates a futuristic Los Angeles made up of Asian, European and Central American influences. Terry Gilliam's *Brazil* (1985) was a retro-futuristic piece with ideas coming from 1930s publications of new inventions.

ABSTRACT AND SURREALISM

Applying an abstract quality to a set through lighting or the quality of the film/camera/video production can dramatically enhance the feel. Abstraction is very effective in helping to illustrate altered mind states. It has a very loose connection with reality: shapes, form, patterns, colour and texture that make you question where you are. It can also emphasize, simplify or exaggerate to alter perception. Designers adopt varying levels of abstraction – full, where very little connects to reality, or partial, where something subtle is changed. Subtle changes can be most effective.

David Lynch is a master of creating imagery out of ordinariness. In a scene from television series *Twin Peaks* (1990 to1991), Leland Palmer has

Task 4: Research Abstract Architecture

Carry on researching abstract forms by going on a photo expedition. Capture imagery that is removed from reality. Consider what makes architecture abstract.

been brought in for questioning over the death of known felon Jacques Renault. The scene is accompanied by ear piercing screeches as we the viewers are in a dark tunnel, but as the camera gradually pulls back and rotates, we slowly realize that it is in fact one of the perforated holes in a ceiling tile in the interrogation room in the police station.

THE TERM ABSTRACT

Screen Designers owe a great debt to fine artists, theatre designers, performance artists and photographers who have experimented visually with ideas that stretch beyond our reality. Experimenting with abstract ideas can be an effective way to express a mood or atmosphere when reality isn't enough to support a narrative. Abstract and surreal ideas have often been used in dream sequences. They are great at creating a feeling of uneasiness because they play with the mind, using imagery that defies logic and consciousness. This works because all of us can recall dreams that are beyond the realms of comfort, sanity and reality.

In David Lynch's *Lost Highway* (1997), the Madisons' house is portrayed as a labyrinth with long hallways and rooms that are difficult to process. This disjointedness is extremely effective in creating a feeling of uneasiness in this modern house. The house has narrow windows that create slivers of light that only partially illuminate spaces, helping to build up tension, especially when characters move through the hallways and disappear into darkness. This environment gradually builds tension and suspense at the beginning of the narrative very effectively. Sinister videotapes keep appearing on the front doorstep, showing footage of the house's exterior, then the interior, and then the interior of the bedroom when the couple is asleep.

Psychological thrillers and horror films use this form of expressionism to great effect. In early silent films, visuals had to convey so much more to the audience, as they didn't have audible dialogue to help tell the story. *Das Cabinat des Dr Caligari* (1920) was a milestone in filmmaking and production design. It was the first art film ever made that was influenced by German Expressionism, and shot from the disturbed doctor's viewpoint. The asymmetrical sets were painted with sharp angles, distorted perspectives with twisted architecture that conveyed the psychology of the narrative. Dr Caligari and his assistant, who is a somnambulist (i.e. a sleepwalker), use a circus act as a ruse to cover up their murderous acts. Theatrical set design becomes claustrophobic screen design with the use of distorting perspectives that lift the design off the screen

This form of psychological expression has developed in different ways. In *Ringu* (1998), Director Hideo Nakata, and his Production Designer Iwao Saitô, use limited colour and abstract Japanese architecture to create eerie scenes. The shadows that are created alongside the singular surrealist objects, help to build an increasing feeling of dread and fear.

Using different and unusual materials can move ideas away from normality. In Fellini's *Casanova* (1976), Fellini did not see Casanova as a well-travelled aristocrat, but as a consummate womanizer and seducer who seemed incapable of showing emotion. To accentuate this dysfunction, the set design was created with artificial and strangely grotesque caricatures with symbolism of mis-en-scène. The entire production was filmed in studio helping to maintain the artificiality of the narrative. In one memorble scene, Casanova is rowing away from a voyeuristic tryst from the mainland on a stormy sea made out of billowing plastic sheeting – creating an effective and symbolic vision.

DESIGNING FOR STUDIO: THE ADVANTAGES

Studios or sounds stages are they are sometimes called, are soundproof facilities where constructed set and sound are recorded for film, television, music videos and commercials. They are specifically designed and equipped for set construction, lighting grids that allow a variety in light placement, and the positioning and movement of the camera.

Designers love working in studio spaces because they can let their creativity flow. As designer John Beard says:

> Studio based films usually give the best design opportunities.
>
> (Ettedgui, 1999, p170)

Because these environments are purpose built, they offer the most conducive working environment in which to create exciting new worlds. For a Designer, total control over a space allows possibilities and flexibility that cannot be afforded on location. With a blank canvas, the Designer can custom build their ideas to their own specifications. This is a clear advantage if there are sets that you have no hope of ever finding on location.

Working in these spaces allows unlimited shooting time, provided the budget and scheduling allow. The crew can also control all aspects of the filming/recording process, such as lighting, sounds and camera movement. It is a great advantage during pre-production, production and postproduction – all departments are on site close to the sounds stages, allowing for quick changes and adjustments. It also gives you the flexibility to experiment with dressing and set, lighting, action and shooting. This controlled environment is integral when using special effects and CGI (computer generated imagery), where scenes need to be shot with great precision to achieve quality material for the animators. Being able to create different-sized sets in studios can help enhance the narrative. In classic drama, such as Alfred Hitchcock's *Rope* (1948), the set was created so that the camera could maintain uninterrupted tracking shots – something that would have been very difficult to achieve on location.

In *Wait until Dark* (1967), most of the story was shot in a small intimate interior of an apartment owned by a happily married couple. The husband returns from a business trip with a gift for his blind wife, played by Audrey Hepburn. The gift attracts unwanted visitors, and soon she is trapped in an environment that was once safe. The set manages to comfort, confine and contain her. Her home is invaded, yet she turns the familiar surroundings to her advantage, adding excitement and terror.

COMPUTER GENERATED IMAGES (CGI)

Blue and green screen technology is best achieved in studio. The level of accuracy and precision needed to capture the raw data is immense, so the controlled environment of a studio is the best way to motion capture.

DESIGNING FOR STUDIO: THE DISADVANTAGES

In the UK, the cost of renting studio space can be prohibitive, especially for independent and lower budget productions. Sometimes smaller productions are overlooked in favour of bigger ones that will be able to rent the facilities for longer, earning the studio a more lucrative profit. The other main difficulty of working in studio is re-creating authenticity. You might think that it is quite easy, but it is more difficult than you imagine, especially when attempting to re-create wear and tear. This is where an eye for detail is very important. Forging a strong working relationship with your DoP is equally important, as lighting can help achieve realism, as Eve Stewart points out:

> The relationship with the DoP is critical… you are essentially bringing to life and enhancing their vision.
>
> (Interview with author, 2011)

Artificiality is sometimes intentional – to create subliminal narrative, and this can be achieved better in studio, rather than on location. Fellini's *Casanova* was filmed entirely in studio (Cinecittà) in Rome to capture the mis-en-scène. Sets were created in great detail in an almost theatrical artificiality to emphasize the themes of the narrative.

DESIGNING FOR LOCATION

Working with locations can bring realism and credibility to a story that would otherwise be difficult to achieve in an artificial setting. Idyllic locations can have a profound effect on the storytelling. For example, the layout of the actual town that represented the fictitious town in *Chocolat* (2000) enhanced the feeling of small town values and mentalities; and emphasizes how the inhabitants react to the arrival of the free-spirited Vianne and her daughter. The closeness of the buildings and the layout helped to create an environment where an alternative way of thinking was discouraged.

In the BBC's production of *Pride and Prejudice* (1995), Designer Gerry Scott discusses the reasons why they chose to shoot the majority of the series on location as opposed to studio:

> Our aim was to film as much as possible on location because we wanted to use the English landscape as a player in the film. It makes a great difference if you can see real exteriors outside the windows of rooms; it gives a true sense of the geography of the places.
>
> (Birtwistle and Conklin, 1995, p. 37)

Working on location can be beneficial for low budget projects that have smaller crews and more flexibility. For example, *Paranormal Activity* (2007) was shot in the director's home to cut costs. Selection and combination can help tell a story. There are so many possibilities for shooting on location, you can choose places that are ideal, and aren't recognizable. Locations can also be used as substitutes, when the original locations are not feasible to use or not historically correct. For example, in period productions, locations are substituted when there are too many modern buildings and the surroundings make it difficult to achieve the illusion.

ON LOCATION: THE DISADVANTAGES

As much as location can be a great advantage, adding realism to a story, there are a number of factors that you should consider carefully. Even though costs can be low, there are some disadvantages, especially behind the camera. Depending on the location and budgetary constraints, you need to think about basic facilities for a successful shoot, such as toilets, changing facilities for crew and cast, accommodation and transport, to name but a few.

When shooting overseas, productions travel light. This is because the employment laws in various countries, allow only heads of departments to travel. Next time you watch a film or television drama, look at the credits and observe the number of different crew units based in various countries.

When filming on location, you don't have complete control over your environment. This is a challenge for designers, as they have to work with what already exists. And because it is a public or a private space, you have to ensure that it can revert back to its original state after the shoot. It is crucial for a Production Designer to visit locations with the director and the DoP and the Location Manager/Scout, who will be able to explain the creative and practical limitations of the space.

Working in a uncontrolled environment you are at the mercy of everything; weather, changes in light, times of day, the seasons, crowd control, external disturbances such as airplanes, nature and traffic noise, to name a few! An excellent example of a difficult shoot is captured on camera in the documentary, *Lost in La Mancha* (2002). Directors Keith Fulton and Louis Pepe followed director Terry Gilliam and his production crew as they tried to make the ill-fated *The Man Who Killed Don Quixote*.

It documents all the physical obstacles that the crew came up against while filming on location in Spain. From jet fighters flying overhead to torrential rain and floods that nearly washed away the sets and expensive equipment, it illustrates the extreme difficulties of shooting on location, and shows how continuity is more difficult then it seems. For example, after the rain the soil changed colour and didn't match the frames taken at the beginning of the day, ruining the continuity. It gives valuable insight into the art of film making, showing the detail, and painstaking effort taken to achieve a vision.

Task 5: Create a Shoot on Location

To experiment with location selection, choose a short story or extract from a script, and limit yourself to locations only. See if you can select a series of locations, which, when put together create a believable story.

CEMENTING ILLUSIONS

For a Designer, one of the exciting and challenging parts of the job is the chance to create scenes that work together harmoniously. Observation skills need to be implemented in maintaining illusions. For example, a studio built interior needs to work with its location exterior. Therefore, whatever characteristics the location building has, for example size and shape of windows, materials used, must all be taken into consideration when building the interior. The layout must be carefully planned so that it corresponds with the exterior shots. Architectural details have to be included in the studio interiors to give it credible realism.

On the set of Mikael Håfström's *Derailed* (2005), each floor of the interior of the Schine's family house was constructed on different sounds stages at Elstree Studios in London. To help maintain the illusions of different levels, the scenic painters created scenic backings that kept the illusion of being an actual house. On the ground level, if you looked out of the windows, you would see faint tree trunks, and on to the first floor, the outside view featured branches. At the top of the house you could see the tops of trees and blue skies.

Even the weather has to be realistic – inside and out. The rule of thumb is, whatever is happening in that particular scene's exterior/location shot has to be illustrated in the interior. For example, a torrential rainstorm outside needs to feature on the windows in the studio setting – whether it is physical water or CGI enhanced.

When you next watch a film or television drama, try to work out what is studio and what is location… you may be surprised!

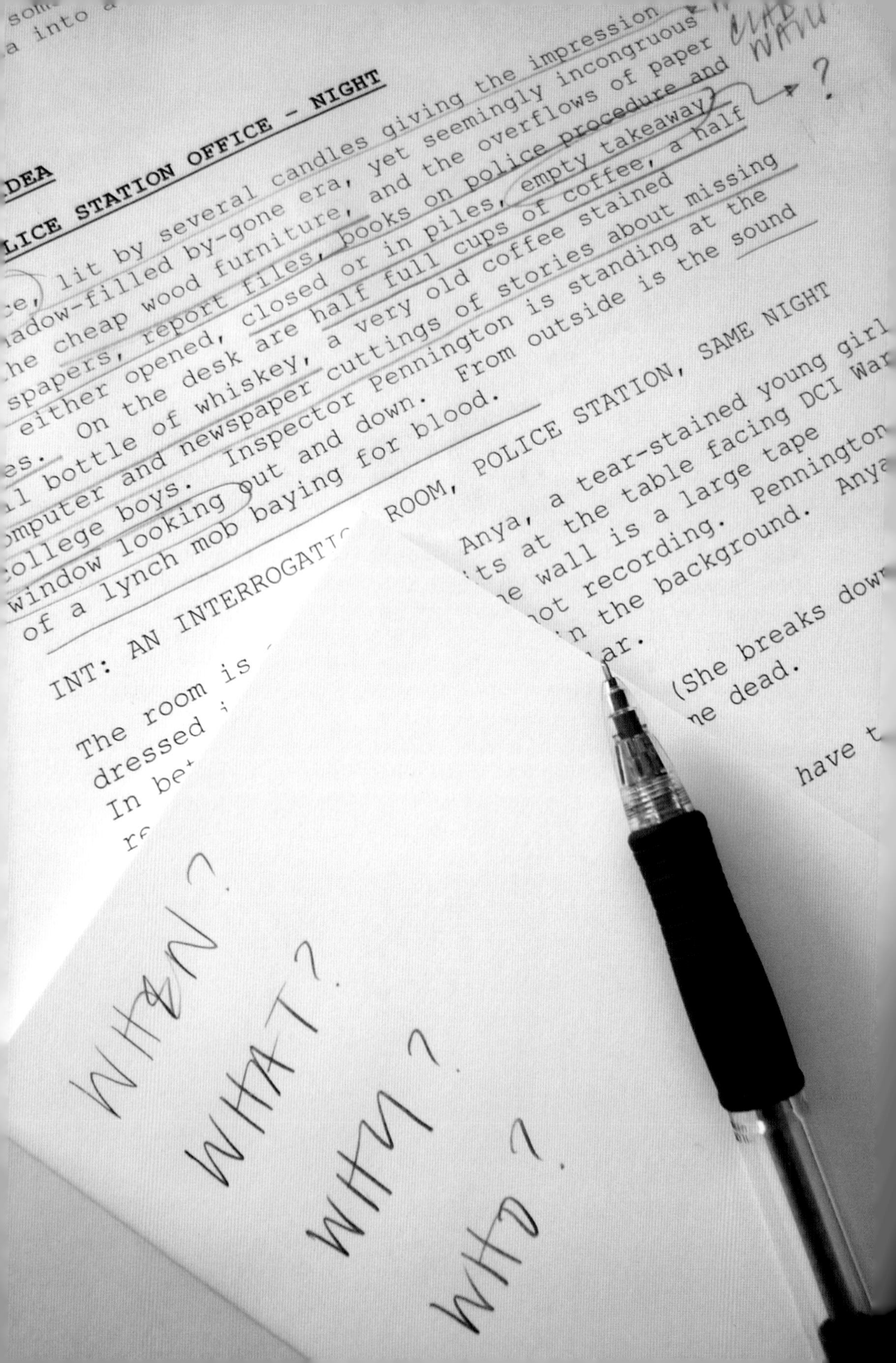

IDEA

..LICE STATION OFFICE – NIGHT

..e, lit by several candles giving the impression
..adow-filled by-gone era, yet seemingly incongruous
..he cheap wood furniture, and the overflows of paper
..spapers, report files, books on police procedure and
.. either opened, closed or in piles, empty takeaway
..es. On the desk are half full cups of coffee, a half
..l bottle of whiskey, a very old coffee stained
..omputer and newspaper cuttings of stories about missing
..college boys. Inspector Pennington is standing at the
..window looking out and down. From outside is the sound
..of a lynch mob baying for blood.

INT: AN INTERROGAT.. ROOM, POLICE STATION, SAME NIGHT

The room is ..   Anya, a tear-stained young girl
dressed i..   ..ts at the table facing DCI War..
In bet..   ..e wall is a large tape
re..   ..ot recording. Pennington
                                 ..n the background. Anya..
                                 ..ar.   (She breaks dow..
                                                  ..e dead.

                                                          have t..

Handwritten: WHU WHU ? ? (with arrow)

Handwritten notes: WHEN? WHAT? WHY? WHO?

3 The Script

TEXT ANALYSIS

Understanding a script or musical promotional treatment is one of the most important parts of a Designer's job. The ability to establish the plot and its meaning is something not to be underestimated nor overlooked. By carefully analysing the text, its direction notes, story and dialogue, the Designer can extract important design information, observations, subtext, and its characters. These elements help form the basis for any story's unique design journey.

The structure of a script or treatment fulfils two important purposes. The first is to tell the story through narrative, action, dialogue or lyrics. The second is to use is it as a strategic tool that forms the foundations on which to schedule and organize the budgeting needs for each department – both of these purposes with be discussed later on in this book.

The purpose of analysis is to have a good understanding of the script, and a good base on which to build solid creative concepts. If the script or treatment is not fully understood, the design can become a direct interpretation of the text, creating nothing more than one-dimensional storytelling, something to be avoided at all costs.

OPPOSITE: Fig. 25 The script of *Trouble at Home* by Jacqueline Shorter.

Through understanding the source material, the Designer opens up different avenues for research and exploration. Even though a designer's aim is to avoid clichés and repetition, it is not always possible to avoid them. For example, imbalances between visual language and storytelling occur in the production of film, television and music videos more so than in commercials. Commercials have a different purpose as they promote products with significant and specific branding, targeting key groups of people – this is where repetition and cliché thrive. Whereas music promos can be typecast by the genre of the music, the lyrics and the artist. In production for screen and television, imbalances can be subtle or blatant.

Watching a drama on film or television for most viewers is a form of enjoyment and many films fulfil that criteria, but how many films can you say are well balanced? Do all the elements work hand in hand, each one complementing the other? We will all have most certainly seen productions that have overcompensated in some way, most often a strong production design overshadows a weak story. The ability to add strength, conviction and distractions to a weak script is a Designer's great strength. In some cases it will be a conscious decision to shift the focus from narrative content to visuals to make the production work and turn a profit! Adding more depth and emotion, through design, can really bring a story to life.

Next time you visit the cinema or watch a drama on television, try to analyze why you enjoyed it. Was it because of the compelling plot, or was it beautifully shot with mesmerizing design? Or was the design so strong that you were seduced by it, more so than the story? Give yourself some time to reflect then ask yourself what you remember about it. If your response is the design rather than the story, then you will have discovered its weakness.

The overcompensating of the visual language may diminish the effectiveness of a narrative but it has the opposite effect for music promos, as a visual medium captivates its audiences in a different way. The power of its design is controlled by the music, its lyrics, its genre, duration of the track and the personality of the artist. The average length of a music video is three minutes, making it ineffective to use subtlety, whereas in non-musical drama, more time is available to create, and gradually build up ideas.

MUSIC VIDEO

The script or narrative of a song is the lyrics. The lyrics tell a story, and along with the music, can be extremely powerful. The music promo's story is more expressive and lively because of its limited duration. A lot has to be conveyed in a very short period of time, which opens up possibilities for experimentation, innovation and cutting-edge design. The medium reflects the current music scene and its fashion and trends, provides a vehicle where new experimental ideas are tried and tested. A promo is like a short film, where a lot has to be said in a short amount of time and abstract ideas can work successfully. The beauty of promos is the flow of the action, which is in keeping with the sound, rhythm and the tempo of the music.

The following example below shows how a designer might receive a music promo treatment.

STRUCTURE OF A MUSIC PROMO TREATMENT

The structure of a music promo treatment contains information about the song such as:

- *Song:* The title.
- *Performer:* The performer's name and the artist. Note: These may not be the same person. Cover versions are as prevalent in the industry as original songs are.
- *Concept:* This will outline the themes and ideas that aim to be put across – the essence of the song's drama.
- *Narrative:* The story that is being told.
- *Locations:* Where the narrative is to take place – interior or exterior.
- *The artist/style:* What is the performer like? Do they have a distinctive look? How do they like to present themselves?
- *Make-up/costume:* Ideas for the artist. These will fall in line under the overall concept.

From this brief, a designer will have a good idea of how to move forward to achieve what the director and artist wants.

WORKING WITH YOUR SCRIPT

If you do have the opportunity, it's worth sitting in on a run-through or practice with the actors and the Director. It will help the story come to life for you, and it's good to see the characters for whom you are creating an environment. Whether this happens or not depends on how the director works, and whether the designer can spare the time.

When reading a script, a Screen Designer should try to remain open and flexible for the transition from page to screen.

HOW TO READ A SCRIPT AND TREATMENT
The script is the starting point of the realization for

any dramatic work. It is the catalyst that sets the production in motion from development to pre-production, and from in production (shooting) to postproduction.

A script is also known as a screenplay, in both film and television. The format and characteristic of a script is very different from a novel or short story. By their very nature, they are drier and, you might argue, less descriptive. When reading a short story or an extract from a novel, the author will be presenting his or her point of view. They control the way the visual picture is built up for you. With their skill in storytelling they guide you through the story with their own observations, visual ideas, taking control over how you use your senses. This differs from reading a script, where the descriptive element is reduced and control shifts from the writer to director to interpret in his or her own way.

The Screenwriter focuses on the story and its characters, making it difficult for first time readers to follow and absorb. If the script is an adaptation or dramatization of a novel, the writer may include key information that is integral to the storytelling… which, in turn, can be very useful for a Designer. A new script can vary and depends greatly on the person writing it. Whichever form the script takes, it is the writer's responsibility to provide as cohesive and as compelling a story as possible so that the Director has a good basis from which to work and creatively develop themes and ideas with the Production Designer and the DoP.

The script is a map that takes the viewer on a journey in an alternate reality. Scripts are typically divided into three Acts. The first Act introduces the setting and characters – this is the beginning. The second Act develops the plot, the situation and the conflicts that arise, and the final act resolves the conflicts and concludes the story. A script is the screenwriter's communication tool for the Director, Production Designer and DoP. It is the map that the production follows to reach its final destination on screen.

Scripts are also divided into sections known as scenes. Each scene captures continuous action and dialogue in a single location. When there is a location change or a change in time, or, in some cases both, a new scene is introduced. Each scene begins with a heading called the slug line, that lets the reader know when and where they are in the story. It informs you whether you, the audience are in the interior (INT.) or exterior (EXT.) of the current location, and also indicates whether it is day or night. The examples below show how these slug lines are presented:

```
INT. BATHROOM - EARLY MORNING or EXT.
STUDY - NIGHT
INTERIOR or EXTERIOR LOCATION - TIME
OF DAY
```

The nature of a script is to contain only what can be caught on camera allowing room for the Director, Production Designer and DoP to add their expertise to bring it to life. The storytelling is always in the present. Even if the story is set in a historical period, the audience experiences the story in its present reality. For example, in Sally Potter's *Orlando* (1992) the story begins in Elizabethan England, where a youthful son of a wealthy landowner catches the eye of the aging Queen Elizabeth. She bestows on him wealth and title on the condition that he never withers or grows old. From then on, the story follows Orlando's extraordinary life, where he leaps forward through time to arrive in the then present of 1990. Viewers share Orlando's journey and become more emotionally engaged as they follow the story.

In *Sliding Doors* (1998) two alternate realities exist simultaneously. The story explores the possibility of leading a double life when Helen comes into contact with the sliding doors of a tube train. This pivotal point sets in motion a series of events, with the same characters leading parallel lives.

The Usual Suspects (1995) has a complex script structure featuring flashbacks that guide the viewer through the story. However it is not always clear whether the flashbacks are real or misleading. This uncertainty creates compulsive viewing. Flashbacks provide the viewer with insight into a character's motivation, and can influence the viewer's emotional reaction to a character. They can also be emotionally manipulative and subjective.

Before the Screenwriter introduces the action, they lay out key information regarding the surroundings; a plan called a *mis-en-scène* (visual scene or storytelling). This French expression describes design for stage and screen. It refers to anything and everything that is visible and happens in front of the camera, such as set design, props, and lighting. It also refers to how characters act and how they move on screen.

All this information is included in the description before the dialogue begins, or when there is a scene change. Some writers go as far as making reference to music at pivotal points; it really depends on how prescriptive the writer wants to be, and how faithfully the Director wants to interpret it. This can be restrictive for the Designer, but the Production Designer's role is to creatively collaborate with the director to fulfil the production's vision.

The extract below is from a screenplay for a short film. Note how the writer provides us with visual clues on the room's appearance, and the type of furniture in it. We know that the scene takes place in an interrogation room, in a police station in the evening. We know that the room has a window and wood panelling. There is a tape recorder that sits on a large wooden desk, two chairs and three characters.

This helps the Designer note specific details

and objects that are integral to the action that is about to unfold. By describing details in this way, the writer helps the reader to form visual ideas about the environment, and provides a logic to the scene in anticipation of the dialogue and action.

INT. STATION INTERROGATION ROOM -
EVENING

A wood-panelled room with a large solid wooden table and three chairs. On the table is a tape-recording machine Police issue — it's not recording. Ward sits in his coat across from an anxious thin, blotched-faced, sandy-haired boy, Anderson, 13. As if in answer to his malnourished appearance he rabidly chews his nails and sweats profusely. He lifts up one long shirtsleeve to scratch his arm. Ward notices the blistered skin and excessive fair hair. Pennington stands by the window, staring out.

                    WARD
You've come this far, son. Don't
back out now.

                  ANDERSON
I just want to say my Dad never
gave me anything he never meant
for me to catch.

                    WARD
Who's this about?

                  ANDERSON
They call him the Mad Magician.

                    WARD
Who, your father?

                    ANDERSON
    No, my doctor.

(Extract from *Trouble at Work* by Jacqueline M. Shorter, 2001 ©)

THE BEGINNING

When reading a script for the first time, always remember that it is the beginning of a new journey into an exciting and new world, and should be treated with respect. Find a comfortable, quiet place where you can sit and read uninterrupted. Some may think reading a script anywhere will give the same first impressions, but, as this is the beginning of a new design journey it is important to focus and avoid outside influences that may distort your reactions.

It is best to establish a good foundation on which to build – so start as you mean to go on! Read your script through from start to finish without making notes, so that you can fully absorb and reflect on the story, its plot, where it takes place and its characters. By this point early images will begin to form in your mind. Ask yourself about these images… what are your initial impressions of and reactions to the story? Did it make sense to you? The first read will give you some initial impressions, reactions, and maybe even influential imagery.

Now read it through a second time. In the second read, you should be absorbing more detail; to further your understanding of the narrative. Begin to make notes about the story, its environment and the characters that inhabit this world. Remember your initial feelings and reactions from your first read, now observe whether your feelings and impressions have changed or stayed the same after the second read. If they have stayed the same, you can move on to analyzing and extracting information. (There will be few times, if ever when you can read a script once and have the whole story worked out. Do not be tempted to travel down this road, as you could miss out on vital information.)

If your opinions and feelings stay the same, ask yourself why, and take note of them. These observations can be anything from a clearer understanding of the plot to changed feelings towards certain characters, or even a different perspective on the environment.

By reading the script more than once, you are delving deeper and deeper into the narrative with every read. A script is like an onion – you need to peel back the layers to get to the core, or the essence. If there are things about the story that you find confusing, make sure you note them down. Try reading the script again and see if they become any clearer. If not, this should be the time when you discuss the script with the Director to seek guidance and clarity. Take note of the things that trouble you about the script, so that you cover all areas. The more detailed the discussions in the initial stages, the better the journey will be for you and your team.

Throughout this book, great emphasis is placed upon the uniqueness of each project. Projects may have a similar feel or genre, but they will never be exactly the same. This applies to all components of a project, including the screenplay… it should always be approached as a unique experience, so that the entire production team can translate it into distinctive imagery and sound. The main aim of any creative project team is to present and tell the story in a unique and visual way. As the characters play a huge part in propelling the story forward, the world that a script's characters inhabit is just as important as the narrative itself. The story and its characters need visual support from their surroundings, evoking the period of time and atmosphere to delve deep into the heart of the story.

EXTRACTING AND ANALYZING INFORMATION

After reading the script for a third time, begin to ask yourself some key questions: When does it take

Script Breakdown Chart

Scene Order	Time	Place	Observations	Background	Mood	Atmosphere	Colours	Texture	Design Ideas

Fig. 26   A basic script breakdown chart.

Production Title:
Script issue:

Location:

Page	Scene No.	INT / EXT	Day / Night	Location / Scene title	Scene description and notes	Specific Requirements

Fig. 27   An art department script breakdown chart.

Production Title:
Script Breakdown:
Breakdown Sheet Number:

Pages	Scene No.	INT / ENT	Day / Night	Script Day

Set Description		Studio
		Location

Props	Cast	Costume

Extras	Vehicles	Other

Production Notes

Fig. 28   An art department script breakdown chart.

place? Where does it take place? Is there a specific period in time? Who are these characters and what is their place in this environment? What in the script gives you ideas about the When, Where, Who, and Why. (Remember the script's *mis-en-scène*.)

Now look at the script itself. How is it written? Does the script give you any clues on what the writer is trying to say? Or how they feel about the story? Does it give you any clues about themes or idea? This may be difficult to detect at first, compared to a short story, for example. In a literary piece writers spoon feed the reader with their opinions through their own observations and the way they describe a particular situation will give ample clues on their commentary.

The structure of the script is more uniform, but the strength of a good screenwriter is how he or she communicates their thoughts and ideas to you. Observe the story, its essence and how the drama unfolds. Notice the locations that are chosen, and the level of detail given to them, also look at the characters and how they are portrayed – prompts such as these will give you insight into what the writer is thinking and feeling, and ultimately their overall message.

THE PURPOSE OF THE BREAKDOWN CHART

Breaking down a script fulfils two specific purposes for a Production Designer – the first is to provide logistical and technical design information that plays a fundamental part in the planning and scheduling process, and the second is to supply the story's visual needs.

Fig. 26 is an example of a simple breakdown chart that is aimed to help a new Designer organize, record creative thoughts and single out crucial information. This chart needn't be shared with anyone; it is purely for personal use. If you use a basic column chart with the headings listed below, it acts as a checklist and will prompt you to note down each scene's key requirements leaving little chance of missing anything. Each sheet relates to one scene. File all the sheets in chronological order in a folder, so that it is easily accessible.

Checklist for Script Breakdown

Scene order/name   The chronological number of the scene. It is also recommended to note the scene name or description.

Time – This refers to day or night, time, the year or decade, the month or season.

Place – Inside or outside. It also refers to the country and city in which the action is set, and its specific location.

Observations – This can be anything that the Designer and Director deem important. Specifics such as particular designs, brands, models and so on.

Background – This refers to the social or political climate. Anything else that is happening while the story is being told.

Mood and Atmosphere – The feeling and emotional connections that the story evokes. It can also include the type of genre, which may be useful.

Colour and Texture – Are there any specific references that are important to the mood and atmosphere?

Design Ideas – These will be your initial creative response towards the story. Careful analysis is vital at this stage.

Figs 27 and 28 are examples of art department industry standard breakdown charts. These vary from production to production, but the level of detail required is the same. Documenting information in this form provides the Production Designer and the team with a clear overview of the project. It identifies potential challenges, the need to find solutions, keep track of the schedule and ensure that it remains within budget. In this way, no nasty surprises crop up. Some projects will require all areas to be filled out. This should be done chronologically, and you should store them in a file for easy access. The chart is not only for the Production Designer and the art department, it is guidance for other members of the production, as it sets out information such as make-up and wardrobe, stunts, special effects and anything else that a scene requires for the action.

Budget management is as important for a Production Designer as designing the sets. Careful monitoring is essential as there are many other teams in the art department that need to be included. The Designer should note the number of scenes, where they take place; whether they are interior or exterior. The Designer is not only keeping a note of the design, but also what else is happening in the environment. The breakdown reduces the script to a checklist for scheduling and budget purposes as well as design information.

Scripts are in constant revision throughout the production process. The Production Designer and the production team must keep on top of all the script changes to avoid wasting precious time and budget on scenes that will never be shot.

ANALYSIS

If you are not currently working on a project, choose a script from a film or television drama that you have not seen. This prevents you from being influenced by someone else's interpretation.

A script has two phases. The first is analysis and discussion and the second is to extract and document. After reading the script you should be ready to answer a number of questions that will lead to in-depth discussions about the story.

The following sections provide a series of questions that should be asked, to acquire a deeper understanding of the narrative.

STORY

What is the story about? Do you understand the story? If not? Why not? What do you find confusing about it? What is the story's drama? Is there tension in the story? If so, what is it and where is it coming from? What are the turning points; where are they and how do they affect the story? (There will always be a number of these in a script. They propel the story forward, change it, and twist it into something unexpected.) What moves the story forward? Is it the characters or a situation, or both? Who are the characters and what are their roles in the story? What is their position in this situation? Is it tension between characters or a third party, or from a situation the characters find themselves in? Do not leave the characters out of the analysis, as they are essential to the production design.

Once you have a good grasp of the story, you can begin to look into the themes. How do you feel about the story? What is your attitude towards it? What is your point of view? What is the writer's point of view? How do these compare to the Director's view?

Is there an overall message or a specific topic that captures the essence of the story? Is there one thing above all else that ties it all together? There may not be just one, but a number of interlinking themes. What is the emotional impact of the story? Does the environment of the narrative reflect characters? If so, how? What's the psychological nature of the story? Is there a catalyst that kick-starts the journey? Does the architecture or physical surroundings help tell the story in a visual way?

THE CHARACTERS

Understanding and getting under the skin of the story's characters is a crucial part of analysis. The Designer becomes emotionally engaged with them, understanding each character, their individual personalities, and how they influence their surroundings. An environment loses effectiveness and context if the characters are ignored. So it is imperative that character analysis is carried out in much the same way, so that a complete picture can be painted.

The following preliminary questions should help you to get to know the characters. Try to approach them as if you are meeting them for the first time. Remember, the audience will have to do the same, so the more information revealed, the more creative possibilities there will be.

- Who is this person?
- What role does he or she play in the story?
- What is this character's relationship with the others?
- How old is this person?
- What is this person's ethnicity and social background?
- Which social class does he or she belong to?
- What is the state of this person's mental health? How does the situation affect it?
- What is this person's style?
- What is their physical appearance; their build (stature)?

You will find that more questions emerge as you go through, which will develop your analysis.

THE ENVIRONMENT

Every space has its unique character and story. Here are some preliminary questions in relation to each environment.

- What is the space like? – Cramped? Claustrophobic? Spacious?

- What feelings does the space stir inside you? Is it comforting? Calming? Chaotic? Hostile? Unnerving?
- Does the space feel warm or cold?

And so on… these answers can lead to discovering a theme or concept evoking a feeling that reflects the unfolding drama.

In this second phase, make sure that you have a number of breakdown charts to hand, remembering that each sheet should only refer to one scene. Observe what was discussed earlier about the structure. The slug line at the beginning of each scene will tell you where you are and when. Note how many scenes the script is broken into, and how many environments there are. The slug line will also tell you whether the scene takes place inside or outside.

- Does the scene take place during night or day?
- Are there specific places that can be identified with a particular character?
- Where do you find the clues about the décor?
- Where does it take place? What country, city, period in time?
- Look at any recurring imagery.
- What is the scene transition like? How does it come about?
- Make a note of the locations and any other elements such as visual and special effects.
- Where are the locations?
- What period of time/time of year/weather conditions? And do these affect the narrative?

The Designer will already be discussing with the production team whether locations need to be built in studio or whether they need to be found.

DESIGN

Details about the look of an environment can be found in the description when the writer is introducing the scene before the dialogue begins. See the example below:

```
EXT: AN ENGLISH COUNTRY VILLAGE -
LATE WINTER AFTERNOON
```

A tightly knit Tudor village, closely hugging an imposing stone church, with its timepiece yellow with age. Slowly the church doors open and the congregation dressed for winter in 1950s' clothing hurries out en masse, quickly dispersing into the early ghostly lit evening, some on foot, others in cars. Only one car speeds away, a brown battered fifties Beetle. It travels up the main thoroughfare of the village, passing by darkened storefronts, heading on towards the façade of a large white and black Tudor house, the Police Station, which faces the length of the street. The car screeches off to the left just before the pale as death 35-year-old face of Inspector Pennington stares out of the window.

```
            PENNINGTON (V.O.)
It was Ward's last case before
he'd been forced to retire. I
should know. I was made an offer
I couldn't refuse. Not that my
partner knew anything about it,
though. Or knowing him, maybe he
did.Top brass always made a big
deal about the prestige associ-
ated with the last case. Who the
hell were they trying to fool.
It was all part of the winding
down of a once sterling career
that had picked up too much
unclaimed baggage along the way
```

```
- and Ward had just been handed
another piece. Me? I was just
along for the proverbial ride.
Hell. Maybe it was the send-off.
```

```
            DCI WARD (O.C)
For God's sake, try and pull
yourself away from the window.
```

```
            PENNINGTON
I don't like it. There's madness
in the air tonight.
        (He pauses in thought)
There's a bad moon rising, Guv.
```

```
            DCI WARD
It already has.
```

(Extract from Trouble at Work by Jacqueline M. Shorter, 2001 ©)

The slug line already informs us that the scene is taking place outside in an English country village, in the late afternoon during winter. The writer then goes on to describes what sort of village it is, in what decade it is set, and what sort of cars are around. There is also mention of landmarks, such as the stone church with its old clock face, and the Tudor police station. The writer also hints at the over all feeling – 'early ghostly lit evening' indicating an uncomfortable undercurrent.

The scene description should not be the only part of the script that you should analyze. Pay close attention to the dialogue and action that unfolds, there will be other important references that need to be documented. Using different highlighter pens, work through the script, highlighting observations relating to atmosphere, environment; the pivotal points at which they change, details of décor and props.

Analyzing a script is an ongoing process, from development, pre-production right through to shooting. As long as you understand the script, and understand the direction the Director is going in, you will be able to adjust, as a film or television or video project will never stay exactly the same as when you read it before production started.

EXPLORING THEMES AND IDEAS

Conceptualization is the red thread that ties all the scenes together, helping to enhance and support the script's or treatment's narrative. Without it, they are separate settings floating about with no anchor. The purpose of a concept is to make all the scenes come together, to be one. It is the visual connection the Designer has with the script that creates uniqueness. The concept becomes individual, and comes from within. It is very subjective – and some productions work better than others.

Singling out themes is a very personal process that takes practice. By delving deeper into the story, you stand more chance of finding its essence. A theme can be colour or textural, or even a feeling that works with the action. Definition – subject, message, topic, concept, mood that runs through a story; the unbroken line that runs from beginning to end. Symbolism, elements that connect the audience – the hook that pulls them in… How do you formulate a concept? What are you looking for? Are there any recurring ideas?

In the film *Chocolat* (2000) chocolate is a metaphor for medicine, a magic that unlocks possibilities. It symbolizes the temptations, but also the need not to deny yourself anything. Juliette Binoche's character, Vianne, is a happy free-spirited woman who peddles small dreams in the form of chocolate. Vianne and her daughter enter this small village with hostile feelings towards outsiders. Chocolate is Vianne's way of showing the villagers there are other possibilities or daring the villages to break with their habits, emphasizing small town prejudices and habits where everyone knows everyone's business and secrets.

Now try putting the methods of script analysis into further practice with the following tasks.

Task 1: Short Story

Choose a short story or extract from a novel, and extract as much information about the environment, design and storyline.

Task 2: Song Treatment

Choose a song and research the lyrics, what is the artist singing about? Can you come up with a concept that works with it?

Task 3: Screenplay Analysis

Choose a screenplay with three different environments, from a film or television drama that you haven't already seen. Analyse the script, and practice extracting information about the story and characters, as well as uncovering details on the themes that run through the story. Find out what the writer is trying to say.

4 Research

WHY DO WE RESEARCH?

Research is an integral part of the design process, and as a Designer it is important to be open to new ways of seeing the world. Ideas appear and develop through research. A Designer should always aim to push the boundaries of originality and to avoid clichés. This may seem a simplistic realization, but it is a Designer's prerogative to be innovative, and to find new exciting ways of enhancing and exploring a story.

One question should always be in your mind when you embark on a project of this type. How does it best serve the story? In the early stages of creative development it will be a good idea to keep this sentence/mantra in your studio space, mount it on a notice board so that it is always visible while you work.

WHERE TO BEGIN

The previous chapter focused on the importance of breaking down the script and extracting key information. This chapter takes that information further, guiding it along the design journey. It is tempting to start building a set straight away, however, by only using raw ideas, you are prevent-

ing yourself from the vast creative possibilities that breathe life into the story.

When these themes and ideas present themselves, the key aim is to emerge from the research process with a stable design concept – one that can be explored and developed throughout the story. This gradual development helps lift the narrative from page to screen – this is only really possible through the physical act of research.

The identified themes and ideas are a fundamental basis for research. Initial or preliminary research is almost instinctual. You will have noticed when reading a script that you are already building up a series of images in your mind through the influence of the action and narrative. It is important to recognize and record ideas and observations and not to dismiss them; trust them, as they will play a crucial role in the process and for the overall design journey.

KNOWING YOURSELF

At this point consider a few soul-searching questions: What inspires me? Where do my influences come from? If the answer is 'I don't know', ask yourself some other questions: What do I like? What do I not like? Now take a moment to look at your personal surroundings, the products you buy, the clothes you wear, the books you read, the music you listen to, the film and television you watch.

Now ask yourself, why do you choose these

specific things and what makes you choose one type of thing over another? The simple answer is personal taste. You may not be aware, but you are being guided by your own personal taste. By asking yourself these few questions, you are identifying your own creative identity. Personal taste is like personal opinion – subjective, but nevertheless very important as it is one of the key attributes that set individuals apart. However, just being aware of one's own personal taste is not enough.

A successful Designer will not only have this ability, but will also have the insight to instinctively know how best it serves the story. When you create something, you become emotionally attached to it, because it comes from within. Because of this, it is very easy to be seduced by it. But a good Designer can make tough choices and objective decisions. Even though the decision process will be yours alone, the challenge is to train your emotional and creative desire. Don't forget, you will be collaborating with a Director who will have his or her own personal taste, therefore, the added challenge is to identify creative ideas that meet both yours and the Director's expectations... something that is achieved through practice and experience.

There are a variety of ways to research, and through practice and experimentation you will find a strategy that works best for you. Libraries are an excellent source of information. There is a wide selection of subjects to choose from. Art and design universities and colleges carry a selection of subjects from fine art to photography, from fashion to architecture and industrial design. If you are not affiliated with an art university or college, visit your local library and find out what selections they offer. They may even be able to point you in the direction of design-specific libraries or shops.

Museum and gallery bookshops are another good source for research material. These shops have a really good selection of publications. There is nothing wrong with flicking through a few books; it will expose you to new creative influences. In addition to books, try to immerse yourself in other forms of creative expression. Exhibitions, such as art and design, photography, multimedia, installation art, theatre productions, film and television, commercials, music videos, documentaries, events, festivals are all relevant – anything that strikes a chord with you. If this sounds too daunting, pick up a copy of *TimeOut* magazine or any weekend newspaper supplement – they almost always have an arts and media section.

Production Designer Luciana Arrighi explains the importance of research:

> I spent much time researching as a student, mainly in libraries and art galleries. My main ease with the Edwardian era was given by my maternal grandmother who realized a child hungry for a past era. My father was especially knowledgeable on Renaissance and Classical culture. So a fascination for past periods began early and has lasted. I regard new and unknown subjects, e.g. glassblowing for *Oscar and Lucinda*, fascinating, and spend much time of my own on research before the formal prep period.
>
> I always bring in art and special paintings as inspiration for the team... and still research in libraries, bookshops, museums, galleries... only use Google as a very useful fast tool, but this being second hand does not inspire nor become part of my background knowledge.
>
> (Interview with author, 2011)

One can never predict where the next big idea is going to come from, so it is vital to keep an open mind.

A STARTING POINT

There are a number of questions to keep in mind when beginning to research. It is important to start training your mind so that these questions become second nature to you. From then on, you will know what best works for you. Begin by asking yourself the same questions as in the previous chapter: When, Where, Who and Why? Below are a couple of sample questions to help focus your thoughts.

WHEN

- When does the story take place?
- Can it be defined?
- Is it historical?
- Is it contemporary?

WHERE

- Is the story based?
- Is it in a city or suburb or a rural town?

WHO

- Who are the players and what are their roles within the narrative?
- Who are these people?
- Are they professional people, do they live in an affluent society?
- Do they struggle to make ends meet?

WHY

- What is the story about?
- Why is it happening?
- Is there a message?

These simple questions are a good starting point to begin the research process.

It may be helpful to follow the script breakdown from the previous chapter. You might find it useful to revisit the text. The script will be a constant source of reference throughout the design and screen making process. At the pre-production stage, the script is a work in progress, and as work begins, the script is ever changing so it is vital that you have the latest version to hand.

PRELIMINARY MOOD BOARDS

A preliminary mood board is an initial visual response to a script. The images come from a gut reaction, and are an expression of how the Designer feels about the narrative. It is not about specific details. Instead, initial impressions, the mood and emotions, the weather/climate perhaps, a texture, a dominant colour or a specific colour range, imagery, even utilizing text such as specific words or phrases in fact, anything that may help conjure up imagery. As it is an early inspiration, it should be a fairly quick process. The last thing a Designer wants is to go into a meeting with a mood board that has taken weeks to prepare, only for the Director to dismiss its content and go in a completely different direction.

As mentioned before, remember that throughout the design process the Designer rarely works in isolation. However, this early stage is a chance to bring your own ideas to the table. The Director has the final say if the concept is in keeping with his or her vision. However, this is a good opportunity to contribute creatively or even persuade the Director to consider ideas that will enhance that vision.

This can be done before the actual meeting, or after a brief discussion, ensuring that you are not completely influenced by the Director's thoughts and ideas, but more importantly, it helps to know what drives the story for the Director, ultimately helping you progress in the right direction.

Before constructing a mood board, research and collect inspirational images. Begin to think laterally, and cast your net wide. Look at all aspects of design, for example: 3-D, product, graphic, industrial, fashion photography, reportage photography, sculpture, painting architecture, events and so on. This material can come from anywhere: magazines, library books, the Internet and textiles. Drawings aren't necessary at this stage, but if you have initial impressions that complement the research – put them in. It is important to realize that this is not meant to be a pretty picture – it has a specific purpose, and is a tool for the Designer to communicate ideas to the Director.

Task 1: Create a Preliminary Mood Board

Step 1: Themes and Ideas
Decide which themes and ideas are the most meaningful to you (and the most important for the Director). Note that some may be interlinked or sub-themes. If this is the case, choose the most important. It is important not to discard the sub-themes, as these will become important when you do further research at the next stage.

Step 2: Subjectivity
Now consider your personal connection to these themes. Can you associate them with imagery, such as colour, texture, or form?

Step 3: Research
Begin researching. Try to keep your personal taste within the boundaries of serving the story. Start by looking through magazines. Consider other forms of imagery, for example: nature, reportage photography or illustrations. Start to collate your visual research. At this stage, do not question why you choose certain images – trust your instincts, there will be time to ask questions later. Don't forget that this should be a cathartic process that will guide you towards areas for further research. Rip, cut, photocopy or print out images. This stage should not take more than half a day. Remember not to stick anything down yet.

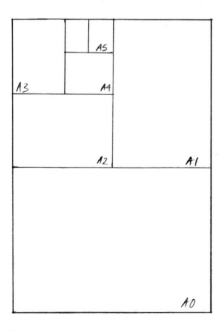

Fig. 30   Paper sizes from A5 to A0.

Step 4: Choose the Background
There are no rules when choosing paper sizes, but an A3-sized (*see* Fig. 30) sheet of either cartridge paper or 2mm mount board or cardboard will be sufficient. Consider the weight of the paper as well. A lightweight paper may be too flimsy and hamper the effectiveness of the finished product.
At this stage, consider the collated research, and ask yourself if there are there enough images for the size of your paper? Does the canvas need to be bigger? Will the background be visible? If the answer is yes, then consider a colour that will complement and enhance the research. Experiment with various shades to see what works best. Introducing a texture can lift and invigorate 2-D research. In Figs 31 and 32, the designer has chosen a textural background to complement the images. The

research is heavily influenced by the seasons, particularly autumn. Using a leaf textured backdrop complements and enhances the quality of the research. Try to keep away from white, unless absolutely necessary, as it can give work an unfinished look, drowning out the visual impact.

Fig. 31 Textural mood board showing soft furnishings. (Designer: Rini Handayani)

Fig. 32 Architectural mood board. (Designer: Rini Handayani)

Step 5: Assess the Research Material
Look the images you have collated. Make sure all imagery is visible on the work surface. Now divide your research into the following groups: colour, texture, form, text, and action images (these could be pictures, painting, photos of character interaction that illustrate the narrative). Decide whether you have sufficient research. If there are key elements missing from the groups, continue to research, but set a deadline for completion, otherwise this process can drag on, and conflict with the production's time table.

Step 6: Themes and Objects
Now that the preliminary research process is complete and all the imagery has been grouped, begin analyzing and creating sub-groups within each group.

Start with the colour group. Can this group be broken down into smaller sub-groups? Start to separate blocks of colour from coloured objects. The blocks of colour will form the beginnings of the colour range/palette or colour swatches. Now consider the coloured objects – what is important about these images? Why you were led to them? Do the images relate to certain scenes or interactions in the story?

Now consider the subject matter: are the coloured objects details from the interior, exterior or from the natural world? By dividing up the images in this way, you start to define and illustrate the story's mood.

Use the same criteria with the textural group. Assess the imagery and repeat the process by removing the blocks of texture and pattern. These could be a textile or textured material as well as printed images.

Define the remaining pictures by dividing them up into the same sub-groups – interior, exterior and nature.

Now begin analyzing the group of form imagery. Divide them into objects and structures. As before consider what each image is, what is its form? Is it from the natural world (human, animal, plant, or mineral)? Or is it an object (this could be an object mentioned in the script or possibly dressing for the visualized environment) or an architectural form. This could be an abstract form that illustrates the story or has a more physical or literal presence, such as a type of building or a style of architectural detail, such as the shape of a room or the details on a pillar for example.

Action imagery will be illustrative of the story being told. Consider whether the imagery reflects a character's expression, a feeling, the situation or both. By using text, or a phrase from the script, you can enhance the action and essence of the story. Return to the script, and pick out one or two key words or sentences that sum up your impression of the piece.

Step 7: Creating the Mood
In the previous step, we looked at the themes and objects. In this step, the themes and objects are connected to the story. Assessing the groups: colour, texture, form, text and action imagery, use the research to tell the story. Begin with the colour group – is the colour palette indicative of the story? For example, can you visualize the drama taking place in the colour range? Or is there a predominant colour, with a secondary palette? Do they complement or contrast each other? Or do they develop from one colour state to the next, enhancing the storytelling? Now consider the texture group – are there particular textures that illustrate the mood? Are there textures that represent a pivotal point in the story? Or do they illustrate something specific? Continue with the same analysis of the form group – do the images illustrate the story or set a particular scene?

These groups create the basis of your mood board. The text and action image groups add the narrative layer to the mood. By only using colour, texture and form – you are creating a mood board that will be non-specific to the story it is illustrating. The images need more to put it into context with the story, and that is why adding action images and text help set the scene for the storytelling to begin.

Step 8: Positioning Images
If you haven't chosen a suitable background yet, do it now. Choose a shade that complements your collated imagery.

Begin dividing up the paper or card into segments that cover the Where, When, Who and Why sections. Consider your starting point and the direction in which it progresses. Don't forget this is also a communication tool. It will be a visual aid when you present your research and ideas to the Director, and will help you to guide your thoughts in a clear, comprehensive way.

Begin by arranging the research within each segment, starting with the larger images, and then placing the smaller ones on top. For example, in the Where section, place scene setting imagery, such as storm clouds, or an image of a house in the midst of a mountain range, and so on. Remember, it is not necessary to use all the images you found. Choose the most effective descriptive images and discard the rest. The last thing you want is for your hard work to be diluted by a mass of images, when a few will do a better job. Now consider working in the colour and textural palettes in an aesthetic way along with the action/character imagery.

Finish off this step by arranging the words or phrases against the most appropriate images.

Step 9: Secure the Images
Before gluing all the pictures to the background, check that you are happy with your choices. Depending on the complexity of the mood board, you could take a digital picture, so that you can replicate the look exactly.

Use the most appropriate glues for your background. If you use thick cartridge paper (290gsm or higher) use a stick glue. Avoid PVA, as it is a water-based glue and paper absorbs it easily, leaving research looking warped and crumpled. If your background is 2mm cardboard, use stick and multi-purpose glues. You can use PVA sparingly. When gluing images, make sure that all the edges are glued down. Don't forget that this is not only a communication tool, but, a piece that reflects your creativity so, it should look as professional as possible.

Step 10: The Finishing Touches
If you have struggled through the last nine steps with imagery that you're not entirely happy with, now is the time when you can do something about it. You can still manipulate the research, and mould it into a form that captures what you really want to say. Try drawing on images or altering them using pencils, pens, chalk, paint or acrylic inks to get exactly the effect that you want.

Most libraries have black and white photocopiers and some have colour copiers. Take copies of anything that inspires you, but remember that any published material has a copyright. This means that it is only for your own personal use.

Do's and Don'ts

Do:
- Experiment with different ways of showing mood board inspiration.
- Experiment with different textured backgrounds.
- Try to achieve specific themes/ concepts through the mood board. For example, if the story's narrative is very structured or rigid, adopt the same feel when presenting your research.

Don't:
- Be tempted to overload the mood board with images.
- Choose overpowering colours for backgrounds. No matter how effective the research, if the work is mounted on too striking a colour the impact will be lost.
- Stick imagery on both sides of the mood board. This makes it very difficult to discuss your thoughts and ideas, and can look less professional. It is always best to view all research side by side.

HOW TO PRESENT

When presenting research and mood boards, make sure that you go into the meeting prepared to talk about the work. It may be helpful to write a few notes or prompts. Most importantly, use your mood board. Think carefully about what you have to say and try to organize your thoughts and ideas. It is natural to get nervous in this situation. Practise ways to keep calm. The key is to be prepared and confident with your ideas.

Begin with what initially interested you about the story, and explain the importance of the themes you chose. Use the mood board to help illustrate and support the origins of your ideas. Don't be flustered or offended if you receive criticism or questioning. It is quite normal for a Director not to share all your ideas and don't forget that this is the beginning of the working relationship and a collaborative process. The way the mood board has been constructed should help organize your thoughts.

Be enthusiastic – remember you are selling your ideas. If you aren't enthusiastic about your own work it is difficult for anyone else to be. Try to turn negatives into positives. If the Director mentions something that you haven't covered, simply say something like: 'that's a good point, I'll look into it', and then move on. Ideally, try to maintain as fluid a presentation as possible. You cannot stop people from asking questions, especially if they don't understand where you are going, but try not to lose your train of thought. You can always discuss the points afterwards. This gets easier with practice and experience, and you will be able to brainstorm while presenting. Make sure that you have a notebook with you, so that you can take down any key points and areas that need more attention.

DETAILED RESEARCH

Detailed research takes place after the Designer and the Director have found some common ground – and decided how to move forward. This level of research is much more specific than the preliminary research and mood boards. At this

Fig. 33
Detailed
mood board
– interiors.
(Designer:
Fernanda
Salloum).

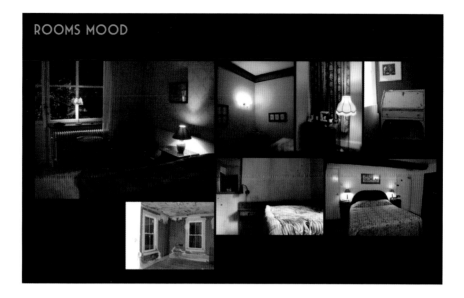

Fig. 34
Texture detail
– wallpaper.
(Designer:
Fernanda
Salloum).

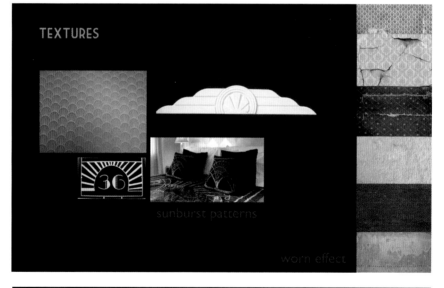

Fig. 35
Colour
palette.
(Designer:
Fernanda
Salloum)

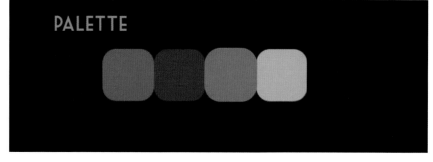

stage the Designer is looking for more depth and more specific things (Figs 33 to 35). For example, the colour palette may still be red, but what shade of red? Maybe there is a texture that is solely connected to this particular shade of colour? This is also where you delve deep into the story, the When, Where, Who and Why sections.

The story will be set in a specific place and time, a time that may have or have had pivotal political and social events in its history. Ask yourself if the issues of the day impact the story or inhabit the characters in any way. Look deeper at the characters and their social standing. Try and find an emotional connection (by this stage you should have a very clear direction), something that will enhance the story and help the viewer to empathize with the characters.

Beginning in this systematic way will allow one idea to lead into another and so on, leading you deeper into the storytelling. Make a note of all the areas that need more research – a lot of the information that is extracted from the script in the previous chapter will become more relevant at this stage. By looking at a specific time and place, you are already painting a picture for the story. Look at the mood board again – apart from the overall mood, are there any specific things that you can take further and explore? Begin to build a checklist of areas that should be explored, starting with the When, Where, Who and Why sections. Has the Director decided that it will be set in a different era to the original script? What is the connection between them for it to work in this alternate time? For example, in Baz Luhrmann's *William Shakespeare's Romeo and Juliet* (1996) the original story was set in Italy, in a city called Verona in the 1600s. Luhrmann transported the story successfully to modern gang culture, where powerful gangs fight on the streets. Men defend their honour with a gun instead of a sword, and yet the original themes of love, revenge, friendship and honour are maintained.

Working on *Morvern Callar* (2002), the detailed research period was a very important process for Production Designer Jane Morton and Director Lynne Ramsay:

When working on *Morvern*, we worked through it in a very a practical way.

Lynne (Ramsay) and I collected nearly 500 photographs per location. We were inspired by photography through to painting... you could see how design could cross over into cinematography. Both Lynne and I came from fine art, which allowed us to avoid stereotypes – we didn't work in boundaries, so there was a lot of overlapping. We collected anthologies of photographic work (fine art) and were inspired by artists like Nan Goulding, Cindy Sherman (Reflective), Martin Parr for colour saturation, Gregory Crewdson (Twilight), Philip Lorca for the hotel rooms, Diane Arbus for the Christmas interiors.

To create a contrast with Scotland [Figs 36 and 37], we used a heightened sense of reality – heightened realism breaking away into more saturation in Spain [Figs 38 and 39]. I was definitely influenced by the difference in the advertising in Spain – created the majority of the advertising....

(Interview with author, 2011)

Begin researching deeper into the social and political events of the time. Explore the generations, inventions, architecture, design and style, characters and their emotions – anything that helps you understand more about the world you need to bring to reality. Fig. 40 illustrates how it isn't necessary to fill a detailed mood board with numerous images. As mentioned before, fewer images focus the importance of the chosen images. Here, the Designer chooses a maximum of four images to sum up the look and feel for this scene. The

Figs 36–39   Stills from *Morvern Callar*
(2002): featuring actress Samantha
Morton, Production Designer Jane
Morton. Courtesy of Momentum
Pictures, an Alliance Films Company.

Questions to Start You Delving Deeper

When
- In which era/age/decade does it take place?
- Is it historical, contemporary, futuristic, or fantasy?

Where
- In which country or city does it take place?
- Is there any reference to a political movement that can be explored?
- What is happening socially at this time?

Who
- Who are the characters?
- Who are they in this political and social landscape?
- Are they based on real or living people?

Why
- What is happening in the story?
- Are there key scenarios that take place in a historical or contemporary time?

research focuses on a fifties office environment, with detailed sketches of a piece of furniture that the Designer wants to pay particular attention to. Notice the colour of the background, which picks up the shades in the research.

It is not always necessary to create yet another mood board for the detailed research. You may find that you spend all your time working on them. If you are working on feature films for screen or television, you may find that you have more time to devote to this process, but you will be very lucky to get half as much time working on a commercial or music promo – where the emphasis is on speed, and short lead times. In these instances, opt for A4 folders with plastic sleeves and fill them with research.

USING AND INCORPORATING COMPUTER GRAPHICS

The use of graphic design packages as part of the designing process has increased steadily over the past decade. They are useful for Designers who struggled with their drawing skills in the past. Scanning rough sketches or photographs into programs, such as Adobe Photoshop and Adobe Illustrator, allows Designers more freedom to achieve a better visual of what's in their heads. Graphics also has the added bonus of hundreds of effects and filters to enhance their work.

If you have access to a design package, scan in a rough sketch, and then manipulate it with colours and filters. Online tutorials are useful and introduce many tips and techniques.

BUILDING UP A LIBRARY

Every Designer should have some form of library: a repository of collected materials. This collection should consist of anything that you are interested in or connected to. Think back to when we talked about personal taste and identity. You will already have started your own collection of magazines and books. From now on, start to expand that library. Include the surplus research not used in this chapter's exercise. You may find they will fit another mood board later. Postcards and film and television stills are also a brilliant source of affordable research. Whether you are searching through a supplier's website or doing an online image search, the wealth of material online is immense, however, this must never be your only source of research.

I recommend you buy an external hard drive

Fig. 40 Multimedia mood board incorporating collage and drawing. (Designer: Rini Handayani)

for the digital and electronic material – a huge amount can be saved from one project. Save your imagery in an organized way, so that you won't struggle when searching through it. Create folders that are easily definable, and then create a series of sub folders within each folder. The following table shows an example of how to lay out a possible filing system.

Throughout your creative journey, be it making a film, a television series, a commercial or a music promo, you will always know more afterwards than when you started. By keeping samples of things used, your collection will increase as time goes on.

Art	Design	Performance
Painting	3D	Film
Sculpture	Architecture	Television
Ceramics	Industrial	Multimedia
Installation	Graphic	Theatre
Photography	Product	Commercials
	Fashion & Textiles	Music promos
	Jewellery	

5 Illustrating your Ideas

VISUAL IMAGES

The use of visual forms to tell a story has been around since the dawn of time. From the earliest paintings discovered in the prehistoric caves, we have always found creative ways to express a feeling, a mood, and a situation.

The term illustration literally means a form that expresses something. In a creative context, it is a visualization that is expressed through a creative medium to capture and explain a narrative. Many media may be used to tell a story, such as paintings, drawings and photographs. Throughout history the illustrated form has helped us discover, understand and connect with life in another time and the way in which different stories were told. We can learn about a person through a portrait: who they were, what they did and what they liked, just by studying the way they are represented.

In the previous chapter we discussed how much information could be presented in a painted image. However, looking at a time involves not only looking at the sanitized face of a period, but also at other, less polished imagery. Satirical drawings and magazines can be interesting and more revealing, capturing caricatures, scenarios, social issues, class and types. This is often a more realistic view of a time compared to commissioned paintings, created to present an ideal, not necessarily the truth. Court paintings, for instance, were required to omit any unsightly disfigurements. It is said that Queen Anne Boleyn, mother of Queen Elizabeth I, had six fingers, but there we have no visual evidence that this was the case.

Each period has its own influences, specific art movements, political situations, and social issues that offer a great deal of insight into a period of time.

The ability to express ideas is a vital part of the Screen Designer's job. Yet not all are comfortable drawing. It is important to experiment and discover which methods work for you, to convey your ideas in the most succinct and effective way. Many elements can help define the visualization of a story: the narrative, subject matter, the message and the scenario you are describing. The way in which you choose to illustrate these elements can be particularly effective, depending which creative media you use to create the visualization (*see* Figs 42 and 43).

There is great power in freehand drawing, breaking away from rulers and drawing instruments and challenging your inhibitions. Human form in action, for example, is not easy to achieve. Observing form can help:

OPPOSITE: **Fig. 41** Illustration by Silvia Ruiz-Poveda Lomba.

If I am struggling to draw a certain pose, I photograph myself in that pose, and take it from there…

(Interview with Tim Browning, Draughtsman, Illustrator and Concept Artist, at Pinewood Studios, 2011)

As a teenager I learned to draw as a fine artist, but when I moved into fashion design my drawing changed dramatically. Every form became highly stylized, elongated and distorted – I had lost the ability to draw what I saw. Through my theatre design training, and lots of practice, I gradually became more comfortable with drawing in proportion again. Acknowledging your inhibitions and challenging them can help you develop as an artist, as Production Designer Ken Adam explains:

…I decided to liberate myself from my inhibitions and the rigidity of my architectural studies. I sketched more freely and in less detail with powerful strokes. As we've discussed, I had a good grounding in architecture, design and composition. Drawing with a hard pencil and a T-square appealed to my pedantic sense, and these beautiful drawings, my early drawings, were a kind of self-defence, really. I was playing it safe. I was inhibited. I was afraid to let go and express myself.

(Ken Adam *The Art of Production Design*, 2005, p. 80 to 81)

A lot can be learned from stage design where the focus is so in tune with the story and the characters. Theatre Designers pick up and reflect a great deal in their illustrations using scenarios, dressing, lighting, and climactic points with the characters to capture the essence of the story. Production Designer Eve Stewart believes this skill is an essential for a screen artist:

I think you are trained with a great understanding of visualizing the narrative in a very distilled way. You learn to tell the story with a single prop or a very simple change of scenery. You take nothing for granted. You also come at every visual with a great sense of perspective and depth…'

(Interview with author, 2011)

Conceptual art or conceptualization art is a form of illustration that is heavily used in all forms of screen design. This type of drawing captures character, detail and form of something that is not yet in existence. It covers all genres and is used to develop forms in greater detail. Many of these artists start life in fine art, graphic or industrial design.

It can be daunting to see the work of professional illustrators. However, if you want to pursue a career in an art department, you need to persevere and practise. A lot of artists are now well versed in computer software, such as Photoshop or Painter, and can combine the two. Established concept artists are embracing software packages to remain competitive and not to get left behind.

One advantage to being familiar with computer graphics is that the DoP can talk to the concept artist in their own language and having more influence and input. In the current climate speed is ever more important. Two years ago, people were still producing drawings by hand, but now 3-D design programs such as Google's SketchUp are becoming the industry standard.

When providing conceptual images, it is a good idea to provide as many roughs as possible so that the whole concept can be shown and discussed in a short period of time. Fig. 44 shows how the artist (SketchUp and Photoshop) has used texture, form, lighting and even shot composition to communicate the ideas fully.

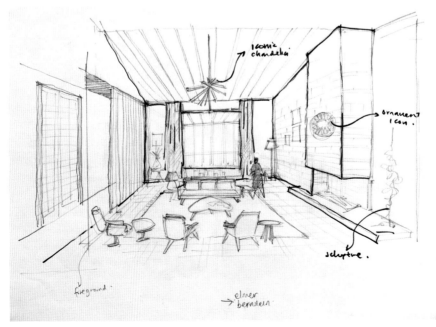

ABOVE: Fig. 42 Illustration using watercolour and lead pencil media. (Designer: Silvia Ruiz-Poveda Lomba)

LEFT: Fig. 43 Illustration using lead pencil and a drafting pen to add highlight. (Designer: Rini Handayani)

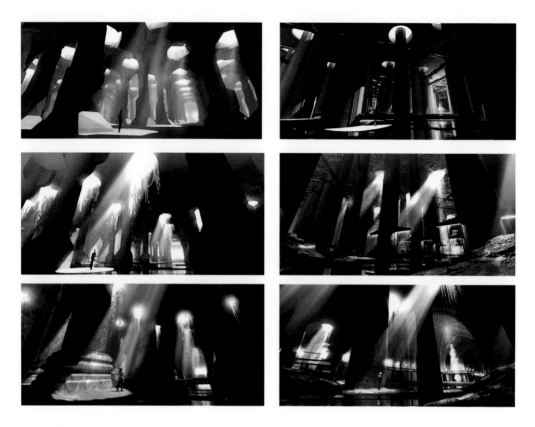

Fig. 44   Rough preliminary ideas of a commercial (2011), Production Designer Simon Bowles, Illustrator Tim Browning. (Courtesy McCann London & Nescafe)

MATERIALS

Visuals sometimes need to be created quickly and selecting the right media can speed up the process. Below is a basic list of media used in screen illustration.

DRAWING MEDIA

PENS

Ink pens and drawing pens come in a variety of colours and nib thicknesses. They can be used on their own or to add more detail when teamed with other media, such as water-based colour ink and markers. Shading techniques such as hatching and cross-hatching help you to add more definition and form.

PENCILS: LEAD AND COLOUR

Lead pencils are the traditional drawing tools. Black lead pencils come in a range from hard (H) to soft (B). The harder the lead the lighter and finer the line drawn, while the softer the lead, the darker and thicker the drawn line, allowing it to be smoothed and smudged to create form and shadow.

Coloured pencils can be very effective on contrasting paper.

Mechanical pencils come in a range of hard and soft leads in a number of lead thicknesses. They are used for precision drawing because of the fine diameter of the leads.

MARKER PENS

There are a huge variety of illustration markers on the market today. Most have two types of nibs, one at either end – fine and broad, so that you can achieve a variety of effects in that colour. Designers like to use this medium as it covers quickly with minimal drying time. They come in many colour palettes from vibrant to pastel shades, making them an excellent choice for quick colour application (see Fig. 45).

PAINTBRUSHES

I recommend you to have a variety of paintbrushes – from brushes for large background coverage to fine detail. It pays to invest in good quality brushes. The better the quality brush, the better the paint application.

PAINT

Watercolour is a water-based paint that has a low pigment content, which gives it its transparent quality. Like most paint media, the designer can control and customize colour palettes for an individual look (see Fig. 46). Mostly appropriate for acid-free watercolour paper, it can also be used on most untreated matte paper and card based surfaces. Being water-based, it is not an effective choice on smooth treated, plastic-based surfaces.

Gouache is another water-based paint medium. It has a higher pigment content than watercolour, providing a much more intense, opaque matte finish. It is a thicker paint and can take time to dry, depending on the thickness of the layer applied. This is also a popular choice as it has a large variety of colour from natural to hyper-intense. It can be applied to most forms of matte card, and paper, and depending on the dilution, can be applied to smoother shiny surfaces, drying to a matte finish.

Acrylic paint is an acrylic polymer-based emulsion blended with pigment. It can be watered

Fig. 45
Drawing
with
illustration
markers.
(Designer:
Leighton
Johns)

Fig. 46   Illustration in watercolour. (Designer: Rini Handayani)

down, and when dry, is water-resistant. It can be mixed with various solvents to imitate specific characteristics, such as oil paint. It has a relatively quick drying time allowing completion in one sitting. Because of its acrylic base, it is a versatile medium that can be applied to most surfaces and dries to a satin finish.

Oil is the least practical medium for screen illustration during the pre-production process as it is oil-based (linseed oil), requiring solvents such as turpentine to be used for thinning. It is a heavy medium and isn't suitable for paper application. It is best used on primed canvas or wood. It has a slow drying time, allowing it to be worked, blended and layered upon. The colour palette variety isn't as extensive as acrylic, and therefore not as popular in this discipline.

Inks come in water, acrylic-based, and indelible varieties. Both water and acrylic-based inks can be watered down. The dilution gives a similar quality to watercolour, and the acrylic provides a more opaque look.

CHOOSING YOUR MEDIUM

When choosing your medium, consider the surface you intend to apply it to. There are many varieties to choose from and each produces a different effect. Neutral colours, such as white or cream (white can sometimes be too bright, and overpowering) may not always be the best choice. Experiment with other colours (try one that is similar to the concept or theme of the illustration) and observe how the background colour changes the atmosphere of the image. If you intend to choose a smooth white sheet on which to draw, choose a textured colour instead. It is important to find out what effects are created with different combinations. Experiment with media that you are unfamiliar with. The nature of the world and the story you are telling will help you choose the right paint medium or media and surface.

PAPER
Think about weight and colour: white, cream, light neutrals, dark neutrals, card, textures, tracing paper, cartridge paper, layout pads, which are semi-transparent and used for quick sketching with pencil or illustration markers.

DRAWING

For a Designer, choosing a subject is crucial to an effective illustration. You are not just painting a pretty picture, but are trying to capture the soul of the story. Designers and their teams produce numerous drawings of varying detail and subject to work out the 'look' and feel of the story. The genre – and the way in which you intend to capture the story (studio, green or blue screen, or location) – will dictate the amount of detail that needs to be shown.

PERSPECTIVE DRAWING – DRAWING FREEHAND AND WITH INSTRUMENTS
Perspective drawings create a 3-D representation on flat media, such as paper for example. The horizon line is our, and the audience's, sight line, and

Task 1: Create a 'Look' through Illustration

Select a scenario, and experiment with varying illustrative techniques how best to capture the 'look and feel' using different levels of detail. Observe the differences in the approaches. How effective are they?

creates angles that indicate where the audience is, whether we can see it from a character's point of view or if we are a third party looking in on the entire situation (*see* Fig. 47). It creates depth of illusion vital for screen designers as it inevitably appears on a flat screen. Positioning the camera to capture different angles creates an altogether more interesting frame. This aspect should be in your mind when thinking about how to illustrate a scenario, mood, feeling and story.

The Rule of Thirds is a useful composition rule. It divides an image up into nine equal segments. The focal point of the composition should be positioned on the intersecting points of the grid (*see* Fig. 48). Doing this adds interest to the image. Using this rule, choose an object and photograph

Fig. 47   The different eye line levels.

High Eyeline
Eyeline

Low Eyeline

Ground Level

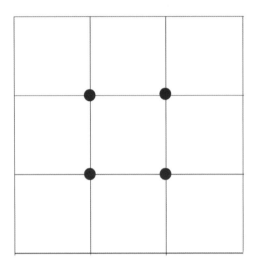

Fig. 48   The Rule of Thirds.

it, framing it in the centre. Now photograph the same object using the rule of nine. Observe the difference it makes to the image.

ONE-POINT PERSPECTIVE

This is when an image seen through a one-point perspective shows a single flat side, front-facing view, where the shapes are parallel and perpendicular to the horizon line. In other words, the surface on which all forms sit helps to create the illusion that when objects are further away, they appear smaller and closer together, while the further away they are the less definable they become. The vanishing point determines the angle at which the perspective will be created, when placed anywhere along the horizon line.

Task 2: Draw a Room Using One-Point Perspective

1. Draw a rectangle that is parallel to the bottom of the edge of the paper. This will determine the dimension and the shape of the room.
2. To establish the horizon line (also known as the eye line or sight level) draw a parallel horizontal line across the rectangle at your desired level (*see* Fig. 49).

Fig. 49
Establishing the
horizon line.

3. Now add the vanishing point. This point will determine the angle from which the viewer will be looking at the space. The point can be placed anywhere on the horizon line. However, for this task you are drawing an interior, so position the vanishing point within the rectangle (*see* Fig. 50).

Fig. 50   Mark
in the vanishing
point for a one-
point perspective.

4. With the ruler, connect the vanishing point to each of the rectangle's corners extending them through. This now gives the angle from which we are looking at this room.
5. To add a back wall, draw a rectangle within the existing rectangle that is also parallel and perpendicular to the horizon line. Make sure that each corner meets along the vanishing point angled guidelines.
6. Now that the shell of the room has been established, begin to determine its features and objects within the space. In this case, a simple coffee table. You have already decided on the angle of sight, so now we need to position the table centrally. Remember that any drawn form in a one-point perspective scale will have a flat side facing the viewer. Draw a simple box in the foreground making sure that it is parallel to the horizon line and the bottom edge of the paper (see Fig. 51).

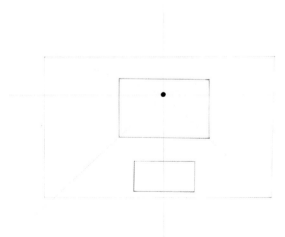

Fig. 51   All lines
begin from the
same point.

7. Connect each corner of the shape to the vanishing point, and then mark in the end of the table, again making sure it is parallel to the horizon line (*see* Fig. 52).

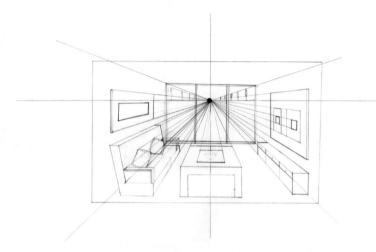

Fig. 52
One-point perspective drawing with guidelines.

8. Continue in this fashion adding objects into the space.
9. Once the base of the drawing is complete discard the guidelines (*see* Fig 53).

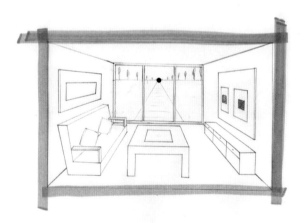

Fig. 53
One-point perspective drawing with guidelines removed.

10. You can also use this method for an exterior. Look through at photographic images in magazines and try to locate the vanishing point. This will also inspire you to try different angles to make the image you draw more interesting.

With practice, you will be able to draw freehand and be able to create more complex scenarios. Production Designer Jane Morton describes how she works in perspective:

> I set up my perspective on trace paper first… scanned it and then work on print outs… it's a great back up.
>
> (Interview with author, 2011)

Working in this way allows you the flexibility to change details, or the look and feel without having to start from scratch (Fig. 54).

TWO-POINT PERSPECTIVE

Two-point perspective features two sides of an object; depending on the eye level you may have three. It is created using two vanishing points that sit along the horizon line. Two-point perspective features objects that show two sides by using two vanishing points positioned along the horizon line. Vertical lines are always perpendicular to it. The key

Fig. 54   Illustration detail on board a galleon. (Production Designer: Jane Morton)

Task 3: Create the Exterior of a Street with Two-Point Perspective

1. Establish the horizon line in the same way as the last task.
2. Mark two vanishing points. In this instance, space them out for a larger perspective image to work with (*see* Fig. 55).
3. Decide the height of the building and the viewed angle, and draw in the corner of the building, making sure that the vertical line is perpendicular to the horizon line.

Fig. 55   Two-point perspective – establishing horizon line and vanishing points.

4. Connect both ends of the line to one vanishing point, then connect the same ends to the other vanishing point. This has now created two sides of your building (*see* Fig. 56).

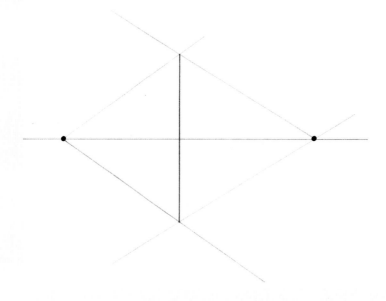

Fig. 56 Creating the perspective, by connecting the points.

5. Now add two vertical lines either side of the guideline ranges to determine the building's width. Once the basic block shape is established, you can create the building's architectural details, as well as windows and doors.
6. To create width of doors and windows: evenly mark out points along the horizon line within one side of the building. Then draw in perpendicular vertical lines from the base to the top of the building, so that there is a series of vertical lines intersecting the horizon line at right angles.
7. Measure the height of the windows along the main vertical edge and connect each point to the right vanishing point. Now that a grid has been created, mark out the basic shape of the windows and doors.

8. Using the same vertical points, connect each point within the left vanishing point, follow-ing the same process (*see* Fig. 57).

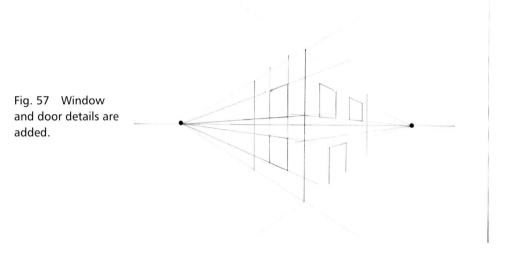

Fig. 57   Window and door details are added.

9. Now that all the basic elements have been drawn you can begin to create the surround-ing environment. By simply extending the vertical edge of the building downwards, you can create the edge of the pavement that the building sits on.
10. You can add more detail, such as streetlights, road markings, trees, people and so on. (*see* Fig. 58).

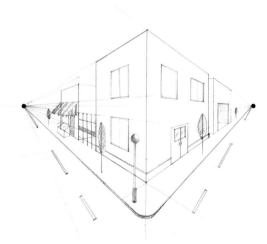

Fig. 58   Vertical line is extended down to create the wider environment.

Task 4: Drawing with Three-point Perspective

The scene can be created from either above or below the horizon line. Instead of two points there is a third.

1. Establish the height of the building, by drawing a perpendicular vertical line (see Fig. 59).
2. When the dimensions have been decided, continue to connect each point to the correct vanishing point, and see how the form takes shape (see Figs 60 and 61).

TOP LEFT: Fig. 59   Three-point perspective, determining height of subject.

TOP RIGHT: Fig. 60   Create the width, always connecting to the correct points.

LEFT: Fig. 61   Adding more detail.

point to remember is that all vertical lines must be perpendicular to the horizon line.

STORYBOARDS

A storyboard visually tells a story through a series of frames that capture the action and move the plot forward. A script may be the basis for a production to exist, but it is its transition to the screen that is its ultimate purpose. As screen design is a collaborative endeavour, the words and dialogue need to be supported visually. A storyboard provides a visual narrative to accompany the words. There are countless ways for words to be shown imaginatively, however it is also the artist's job to help capture the story, situation or idea in a practical way.

A storyboard is broken down into shots show-ing scenarios in chronological sequence. It sets the scene, includes the characters and the action (see Fig. 62). Each frame will visually present the type of camera shot and its movement, the character(s) or object(s), the light, and the direction of the action.

For a storyboard artist, these key elements add impact and meaning to the narrative. The choice of shot and the camera angle can make or break a shot. The storyboard acts as a visual aid for the Director and the DoP to work through ideas and shot set-ups. By working through each frame, you get an overall feel for the fluidity and effectiveness of the storytelling. It also highlights the areas that are less effective and which require more work. An essential part of the pre-visualizing process is time to experiment and discuss ideas. During the shooting stage, there will be little opportunity for spon-

Fig. 62   Coloured storyboard for a video opera, using acrylic inks and oil pastels. (Designer: author)

Fig. 63   Storyboard for a commercial. Original outlines were hand drawn, scanned, then inked in with watercolour. (Production Designer: Jane Morton)

taneity. For speed and efficiency, the crew must know beforehand how scenes will be shot.

The storyboard process happens during the very early stages of pre-production, sometimes called pre-visualization. The Director sits with the storyboard artist and together they work through the story. It gives the Director, Production Designer and DoP a reference base to discuss and agree visual language and style, the lighting and the practicalities of achieving each shot, as together they are responsible for everything in each frame. This process is a way of committing to a creative direction, and ensures that all departments move forward together.

Through the storyboard, the Production Designer will get a feel for how the story will be told, and how the settings will be used and lit. It is a useful reference for the design team. The storyboard is also the source for the shooting schedule; all the information about each camera set up, the duration of each shot, the location, and the action are all worked into the shooting schedule. This is the schedule that all departments on the production work to.

Storyboards range from highly detailed professional industry standard to crude line sketches, but their purpose is always the same whether they are for film, television or commercials. They are a device for communication, a visual guide that all departments refer to and adhere to throughout the whole production process (see Fig. 63).

The world of concept and illustration art can be very daunting. Inexperienced artists must persevere to reach the top, where competition is fierce. Keeping up-to-date with new technologies is essential. Like most areas of screen design, storyboarding is embracing the digital age. To remain competitive, most artists will not only have the ability to draw by hand but be familiar with digital techniques such as animatics – which is a digital moving storyboard program.

New ways to create storyboards are becoming more popular. They can capture the image, mood, lighting, camera angle with greater immediacy, making it a far more effective way of working, if drawing is a struggle. Director Drew Pautz discusses the benefits:

> We did the storyboard via digital camera (which works brilliantly), utilizing of course the fact we were shooting in the house (the Director's home). So Phil Fisk (DoP) came over numerous times and we took all kinds of stills, then we discussed and figured out the shots and assembled them…
>
> (Interview with the author, 2011)

Task 5: Draw a Storyboard

Choose a simple scenario, which includes a few activities, such as going down to the shops for example.

Prepare a series of landscape boxes in the correct aspect ratio dimensions in which the images will be captured. Aspect ratio is the proportional dimensional relationship between width and height. A film in original theatrical format shot on 35mm film will have a ratio of 1.85:1. That means the width of the screen image is 1.85 times bigger than the height. 1.85 = (width): 1 = (height). This differs from images shot in DV (high definition video wide) format sometimes used for television, that is: 1.78:1 to achieve a more filmic effect). Fig. 64 shows the differences.

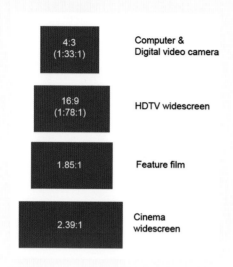

Fig. 64   Screen Aspect Ratio Comparison.

Once the aspect ratio has been established, roughly sketch out the action. Think about how to communicate the scenario visually. Break up the actions into separate scenes. For example, starting inside the house, move to leaving the house, walking down the road, nearing the shop, arriving at the shop, and entering it. Sketch these frames out.

Now think about the action in more detail. Cut the storyboard up, separating each frame, and consider how to fill the gaps. This enables the story to develop and grow. Attention to detail can make a seemingly mundane scenario more interesting.

Expressing action can be challenging, so try researching professional storyboards, and comic strips to get a feel for interesting approaches.

Task 6: Break Down Shots

Choose three minutes of action from a film, television programme, music video or commercial and analyze how each shot is broken down. Observe what happens in each shot: What type of shot is it? What is the camera doing? What is the character doing? What's going on? What's the style, language, feel? How long is each shot, and how does the speed of each shot work with the flow?

Practise how to hold the interest of the audience. Think of interesting shots that can help enhance the narrative, and move the story along.

TYPES OF SHOTS

Each camera shot has a different perspective and feel. It can help convey a range of experiences and emotions to move the narrative on. A shot, its length and the speed with which it progresses can communicate mood and emotion, psychology, movement and style, creating layers to the storytelling. In an interview, *Desire's* Director Drew Pautz explains the importance of selecting the right shots to tell the narrative:

DP: First, we wanted the film to be very simple and use as many long or longish takes as possible, both to try to hold the tension in 'real time,' but also as an aesthetic. That meant that we had to have a very good idea of the action and the shot sequence both for the actors and, importantly, for the edit. We avoided cutaways – again a kind of aesthetic of simplicity – so had to think carefully about the sequence of shots for the story and the final edit.

Second, we shot on a very tight time schedule, so we wanted to shoot the minimal number of set ups possible – within reason. We still dropped shots, but not that many. Luckily to facilitate all this, we were able to work on location with a stills camera in pre-production, and discussed and finalized the storyboard during that process.

GS: Did the look and feel of the story greatly influence the shots you used? If so, how?

DP: Very much so. The film was written to be shot quickly with little money, and the script was written with the location in mind. That meant a kind of useful feedback loop – the feel of the location influenced the story and the story influenced how we would exploit the location. We also felt the script leant itself to exploring difference between light and dark and, fundamentally, between the interior location and exterior – the world of the house versus the exterior world both kept at bay and tantalizingly full

of the possibility of something else. These elements obviously influenced our choice of shots – the back garden wide, airy, but black... versus some of the tighter interiors. In general, however, the story seemed to call for restraint and an objective distance. We decided that the feeling of lonely, dissatisfied isolation in the story was best conveyed through a fairly distant, still camera.

(Interview with author, 2011)

Shots are defined by:
- The distance between the subject and the camera.
- The camera angle.
- The movement of the camera.
- How many characters are in a shot.

The following examples of shot are illustrated through the short film, *Desire* (2010), Writer and Director: Drew Pautz; DoP: Phil Fisk; Production Designer: Gitta Gschwendtner; Cast: Justin Salinger, Denise Gough and Liz White.

Extreme Close-up or Big Close-up (ECU/XCU or BCU): ECU features a section or part of a character or object. It is often used to capture feelings of emotion and detail.

Fig. 65
ECU.
(Featuring
actress:
Denise
Gough)

Close-up (CU): CU features the head and shoulders of a character or a section of an object in detail. This shot can express an emotional connection between the subject and the audience, or an action.

Fig. 66   CU.

Medium Close-up (MCU): MCU includes a full head to mid chest.

Fig. 67   MCU. (Featuring actress: Liz White)

Medium Shot (MS): MS presents the character from the waist upwards. It is a good shot to use to communicate character, and personality. This shot and all the above are good to express emotion, drawing in your audience, getting them more involved in the experience.

Fig. 68   MS. (Featuring actor: Justin Salinger)

Medium Long Shot (MLS): MLS includes the character's full torso down to the knees, and includes the surroundings/environment.

Fig. 69   MLS. (Featuring actor: Justin Salinger)

Long Shot (LS): LS features the character from head to toe, in their environment. It introduces the character in their environment, establishing context.

Fig. 70   LS. (Featuring actor: Justin Salinger)

Wide Shot (WS): WS is scene setting; an establishing shot. It tells the audience where 'we' are within the context of the story.

Fig. 71   WS. (Featuring actor: Justin Salinger)

Point of View (POV): A POV shot is through the eyes of a character. The audience sees the story from that character's point of view.

Fig. 72   POV. (Featuring actress: Liz White)

Over Shoulder (O/S): O/S allows the audience to see the character and what the character is looking at. This can be a very effective shot for creating suspense, as the camera takes on a voyeuristic role, rather than engaging with the subject

Fig. 73   OS. (Featuring actors Justin Salinger and Denise Gough)

Two Shot/Three Shot: A two shot or three shot features two, three, or more, characters together in the frame. Helps to show how they relate to each other as opposed to a single character, which could show isolation or loneliness.

Fig. 74   Two shot. (Featuring actors: Justin Salinger and Denise Gough)

Fig. 75   Multi shot, showing two sides of the story. (Featuring actors: Justin Salinger, Liz White and extras Gitta Gschwendtner, Production Designer, and Leon Westnedge, Gaffer.

Level Angle Shot: A shot is taken at natural eye line, a standard angle.

High Angle Shot: A shot that is taken from above the eye line, looking down on the subject. This can create feelings of insignificance and weakness.

Extreme High Angle: This shot accentuates a feeling of insignificance or defencelessness.

Low Angle Shot: A shot taken from below the eye line looking up at the subject. Making the subject more imposing, dominant, strong.

Extreme Low Angle Shot: Heightens the feeling of scale, where the object becomes even more imposing, dominating and oppressive.

Tilt Angle: The camera moves at an angle to capture action.

Dutch Angle: Used to de-stabilize the viewer, where the camera is tilted in such a way so as to create feelings of disorientation.

Cutaways: These shots focus on nothing specific, but are used to build up mood, feeling in relation to the environment.

Pan: This is a firm sweeping movement from one point to another. This can be used as an establishing shot, or to show an environment through the eyes of a character.

Zoom: The zoom is a smooth lens movement either closing in on the subject (zoom in), or moving away from the subject (zoom out).

Jump cut: This is an abrupt shift from one shot to another, breaking the rhythm of a shot. It can be a useful way of showing a sudden change of mood or situation.

Dissolve: When one shot gradually disappears as another appears simultaneously at the same speed, this is known as a Dissolve. It is an effective way of moving fluidly from one shot to the next.

Fade: This is when a shot fades out; it gradually loses its light contrast progressing to black. A fade in is when the opposite occurs, when a shot becomes lighter from a black screen.

Task 7: Storyboarding

Experiment with a favourite film or television programme, and try to capture a series of scenes through the medium of a storyboard, observing the narrative, action, the camera movement, the type of shot and the duration of the shot

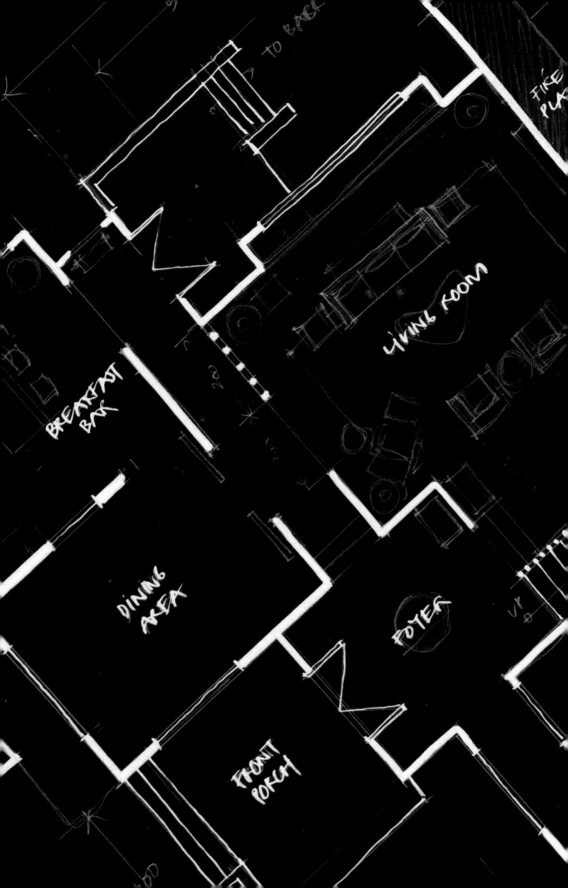

6 Preparation in 2-D for 3-D Realization

UNDERSTANDING THE BASICS: SCALE

What is scale and why do we use it? Scale is the term used to define the size of an object compared to another. We, as humans, build our lives on comparisons.

Observe architectural technical drawings and illustrations such as Fig. 77. The drawings are rarely presented on their own. Buildings are designed to fit into an environment in the same way a set needs to fit a scene or an environment. Understanding scale is an important skill for a Designer. Scaled drawings give accurate dimensions of a proposed set. Working in scale affords the designer a way to communicate with other members of a production. We work in scale everyday. As humans, we compare and contrast everything on a daily basis. By working in scale the Production Designer, Director and DoP can visualize what the set will look like in full size, and how the action in the scene can be played out. A proportioned representation allows for meaningful and constructive discussions within the art department and everyone else working on the production. It is a fundamental and economical way of working through problems that may arise. When working with technical drawings, scale is always present. Working in scale provides a complete overview and understanding of a structure's plans.

TECHNICAL DRAWING

Technical drawing is a universal language that is shared with many disciplines. It is a communication tool for design and construction; the beginnings of the 3-D realization process. It is through this medium that the Production Designer and their art department meticulously work through ideas and problem solving in 2-D in anticipation of

Task 1: Getting to Grips with Scale

Observe the difference when you take a photograph of a building on its own and when you take a photograph of a building in situ. With a building on its own, apart from the obvious architectural details, there isn't much information about its scale. Now take a photograph of the same building, and include its surroundings and passers-by. How do the surroundings affect the scale? See how the image has changed by including people. It is not just a building it is now a building in scale.

OPPOSITE: Fig. 76   Details of a freehand floor plan by Sri Handayani.

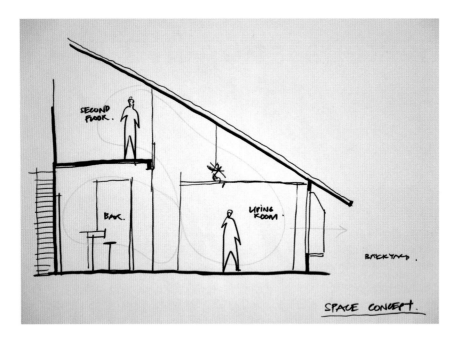

Fig. 77
Architectural
sketch.
(Designer:
Rini
Handayani)

the 3-D construction. Through technical drawing, a Designer can accurately plot out a set's space in minute detail, finding practical and logical solutions to problems. Because of the nature of screen design, the attention to detail is enormous as the camera picks up everything. It is not enough for objects in space to look like they function. Nowadays, they are built with the intention that they must function to maintain authenticity so the level of skill needed is very specific. Each set will have numerous drawings that analyse and communicate each and every detail of the designed space. It is a very prescriptive but necessary way of realizing the design. A draughtsperson will work very closely with the construction and prop making teams to ensure everything works.

Technical drawing can be learned in various ways. One can take a module as part of a design or architecture course. Many professionals take specialized drafting modules, as part of a production design or architectural training course. Others teach themselves by working through training manuals, or learn on the job. Whichever way you approach training, time and practice is vital. Precise legible drawings should convey the correct information and avoid misinterpretation.

When Designers are crewing up for pre-production they will look for competent and efficient draughtspeople who produce consistently accurate, clear drawings of sets and props that work. A draughtsperson should have a good knowledge of construction and architecture, and should be constantly interested in how things move and function.

FREEHAND SKETCHING

Freehand drawing is a good skill to have. It is the means through which a Designer can visually interpret mental pictures. The physical action of sketching helps to formulate, develop and record ideas, and provides the freedom to experiment with different aspects of the physical shape of objects.

There are many advantages to freehand drawing; the main one is its immediacy. When you are involved in a brainstorm session, it is the fastest, most efficient way to communicate and interpret what is being discussed. How many times have you been in situations when someone is verbally describing something, and when you finally see it, it is nothing like you imagined? Sketching can help avoid those misunderstandings and misinterpretations. Words can take you only so far, but drawing moves you on further, as Eve Stewart explains:

> If three people sit in a room and talk about a chair, they will all see a different chair in their heads. If you cannot draw convincingly, quickly and attractively in that meeting you stand no chance of getting the chair you know to be right! Beautiful drawings sell you and your ideas...they also feed your own soul.
>
> (Interview with author, 2011)

Another advantage is that ideas in one's head always work, as the brain distorts them so that they appear logical. However, things may be very different when those ideas are drawn on paper. The physical action of drawing helps you work through ideas in a logical and practical way. Sketching also helps to develop your understanding of objects and space (*see* Figs 78 and 78). Observing the physical attributes, movement, placement and mechanics of an object, can help you draw them and influences how they will be used.

Fig. 78   Freehand perspective drawing 1. (Designer: Fernanda Salloum)

Fig. 79   Freehand perspective drawing 2. (Designer: Fernanda Salloum).

ORTHOGRAPHIC PROJECTION

In orthographic projection, a 3-D object is shown in 2-D form. The physical form and features of the object are shown through a series of views that present each surface area in the correct proportions. Breaking down an object in this way can help you to understand it. Each view provides key information that can be used as a basis for technical drawing. Observe the different views of an object when it rotates up and down, clockwise or anti-clockwise along an invisible central axis.

Different form and dimensional information is available with each view. To get a true physical understanding of the object's dimensional surface area, it must be drawn in a series of flattened views or elevations without perspective distortion. It needs to show the true measurements of height, width and depth. Using solid lines for visible form and broken lines for the hidden, you should have all the key information you need. Depending on the object, there are three or six regular views (known as multi-views) of an object that provide all the relevant information. These are:

- Top view.
- Front view.

- Right side view.
- Left side view.
- Rear view.
- Plan or bottom view.

Understanding the breakdown of a 3-D object and interpreting it accurately in two dimensions gives

Task 2: Orthographic Projections of a Chair

Figures 80 to 85 show each view of a chair. Using solid lines for visible form and broken lines for hidden form, draw six orthographic projections of the chair.

RIGHT: **Fig. 80 Top view.**

BOTTOM LEFT: **Fig. 81 Front view.**

BOTTOM RIGHT: **Fig. 82 Right side view.**

the Designer the basis of knowledge for all technical drawing.

ISOMETRIC DRAWINGS

Isometric drawings differ from orthographic drawings, as they are 3-D drawings on paper that show
three sides of an object or space in true proportion. No corner is shown at 90 degrees and all
horizontal lines are always drawn at 30 degrees
from the determined baseline, with all vertical
lines remaining true or perpendicular. An isometric drawing can be created using the information
from a technical drawing, which makes it ideal for

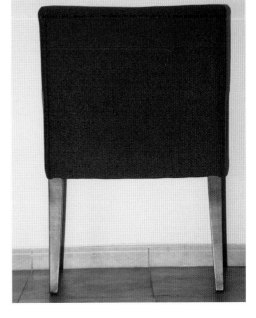

TOP LEFT: Fig. 83   Left side view.

TOP RIGHT: Fig. 84   Rear view.

BOTTOM RIGHT: Fig. 85   Bottom view.

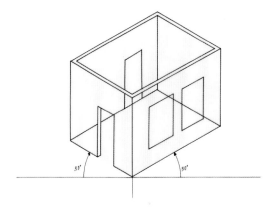

Fig. 86   Isometric sketch.

showing interiors (*see* Fig. 86). These drawings can be drawn by hand or on screen.

DRAFTING LANGUAGE

Technical drawing uses the principles of ortho-

Task 3: Draw an Object Showing Three or Six Views

Select an asymmetrical object and, following the same method as above, considering whether the object requires three views or multi-views and draw them on screen or by hand.

graphic projection to communicate an object or an environment's true form and dimension. Each view provides an accurately scaled and dimensionally correct footprint of the surface plane. In addition to this, each drawing provides detailed construction and design information, including surface detail and types of construction material. The most regularly used views are the plan view, elevation, and section and cross-section views (*see* Fig. 87).

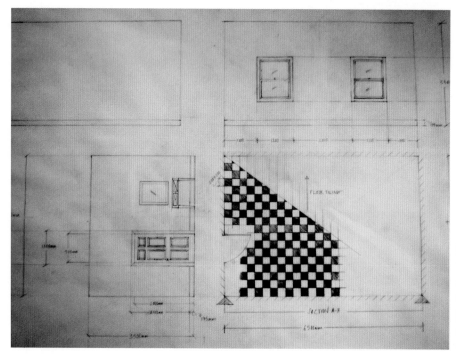

Fig. 87 Technical drawing showing plan and elevations views.

Title blocks are placed at the bottom right corner of each page, providing key information about the drawing, such as the name of the production and details of the Director, Producer and Production Designer. Additional information, such as a description of the drawing, the number of the set it corresponds to, the drawing number of that set, the location, the date drawn, and who drew it may also be added.

PLAN VIEW

A plan view or a ground plan is what is visible when looking at a space from above. The picture plane is never taken from the floor level, but from higher at a height of approximately 3'6" (1m) and 5'6" (1.5m). This means that the drawing will feature all the details and critical construction information that sit flat against the wall, and those that protrude from it. Fig. 88 shows the difference between a picture plane at floor level and above. Notice how much more detail is communicated from a higher vantage point, giving a true representation of the space. Other features will be plotted on the plan, such as doors, windows, staircases, as well as fitted objects such as kitchens, bathroom sets, large pieces of furniture and so on.

ELEVATION

When drafting a set, whether it is an interior or exterior, the front view or elevation is considered a side elevation. When drawing an elevation view, the picture plane is created between the viewer and the facing wall (see Fig. 89). As it is drawn in an orthographic projection, all the details are represented in a flattened manner. In addition, other design and construction details will be added, indicating materials and design such as woodwork or panelling, metal, wallpaper and tile formation.

An elevation from the side provides the vital information about the depth and height of a set and its features, as well as whether the set is

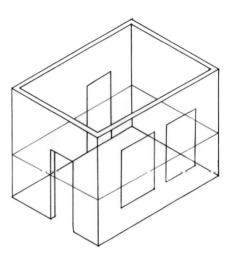

Fig. 88   The horizontal picture plane used for ground plans.

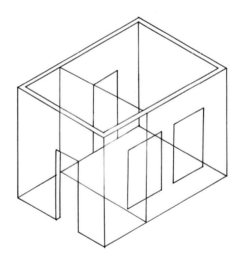

Fig. 89   The vertical picture plane used for elevations.

intended to sit on the sound stage floor or based on a raised platform.

SECTION VIEW

Section views on a floor or ground plan indicate the origin of the elevation. In Fig. 90 the section

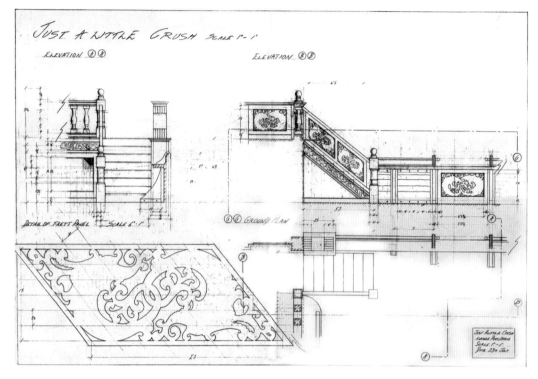

Fig. 90   Detailed technical draft featuring section views. (Production Designer: Jane Morton)

views are indicated by A A and B B. Detailed elevations are drawn larger scale to provide much more information.

CROSS-SECTION

This view shows detail when an object or space is sliced in half. More often then not, a cross-section view will be combined with an elevation. It illustrates the thickness and form of features, such as skirting boards and mouldings.

DRAWING LANGUAGE – SYMBOLS AND SHAPES

A   Centre line

B   Elevation line: indicates where the elevation has been taken from.

C   Hidden features: indicates hidden features and features from above the picture plane.

D   Section lines: indicates the point at which a section view has been taken from.

E   Cyclorama/scenic backdrop – indicates position and shape.

F   Break Line: indicates breaks that don't alter the proportion or shape of an object, but remove a section constant section so that it can fit onto a page.

G   Dimension Line x 2: different ways to show dimensions.

H   Double clad wall: indicates wall structures that have cladding on both sides, when both sides of the walls are used.

I   Single clad wall: indicates wall structures that

Fig. 91
Basic
symbols for
drafting.

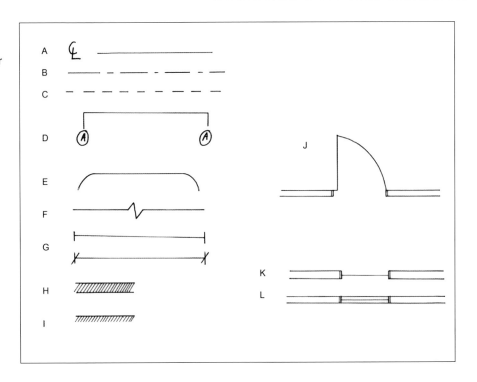

are only used on one side. This symbol is used to indicate perimeter walls.

J   Door symbol: provides the swing range of the door.
K   Standard window.
L   Sash window.

CLADDING

These staples of set design were traditionally wooden frames, with thin layers of plywood nailed to one side for single and on both sides for double. Metal scaffolding braces the walls from behind to ensure the structure is secure. Steel structures are regularly used now, with wooden cladding on top, then worked upon with plaster or other building materials. It is best to discuss with your construction crew how they intend to build certain things, so that you can interpret them into the drawings. This is a good way to understand more about construction.

DRAFTING MATERIALS

PENCILS

For many years wooden graphite lead pencils were the draughtsperson's pencil of choice. They come in a variety of hard and soft leads, and are easy to use. Aim to use three different weights from the range HB to 4H (HB, F, H, 2H, 4H) to differentiate types of line representation. Using anything softer than an HB is not recommended, as the softer the lead, the less accurate the line. The disadvantage of using this type of pencil is that it needs constant sharpening and, depending on the softness of the lead, becomes blunt very quickly.

Mechanical pencils have overtaken traditional pencils to become a preferred drawing tool. They come in a variety of sizes: 0.3mm, 0.5mm, 0.7mm, and 0.9 mm, with a range of refill leads from 2B to 4H. These pencils are ideal for drawing on tracing and drafting media, as the lead never needs

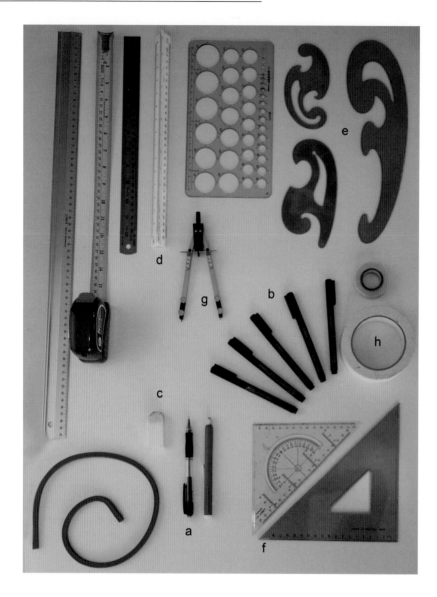

Fig. 92
Essential
drawing
equipment.

sharpening, you simply press the end of the pencil. To save time when drafting, it is best to have three pencils with different weight leads. Just remember, the harder the lead the more crisp and clear your drafting will be. Anything softer than HB is too soft and will lack precision.

DRAFTING PENS

Drafting pens are used in the finishing stages of the drawing process. There are a wide variety of pigment ink pens on the market that come in various nib thicknesses: 0.1, 0.2, 0.3, 0.5, and 0.8. These reflect the different lead weights used in drawings. Pigment ink is difficult to remove, so take care when inking in drawings that have taken hours to create! Ink isn't always used, as drawings need to be updated throughout the pre-production process.

Fig. 93
Scale rulers: A:
Imperial, B: Metric.

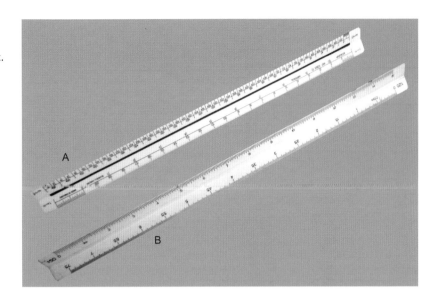

ERASERS

A decent eraser can save you a lot of frustration. Some smudge and don't rub anything out, so shop around for a good one. Most good quality plastic erasers will remove graphite lead from tracing and other drafting media effectively. Don't be tempted to remove the cardboard sleeve at one go, as it protects the rest of the eraser from any oil and grease that may hamper its effectiveness. Refillable ratchet plastic erasers can be very handy for precision erasing. Electric erasers with cylindrical refills are effective in avoiding waste.

SCALE RULER

If we were to draft plans of a set in life-sized dimensions, it would take a very long time and a lot of paper to complete each one – it is a totally unrealistic proposition! Choosing a scale can be as simple as what will fit onto a page. It can also be determined by the level of detail required for the drawing. The architect's scale was designed to measure and draw architectural plans. It features numerous units of measure in either imperial or metric. These scale rulers normally come in two forms: prism shaped (see Fig. 93) rulers, which can feature six to twelve different scales, and its flat counterpart that has four.

If you work in the UK industry, you will be expected to work in both metric and imperial measures, because of the close ties with the North American film industry. Draughtsman and Illustrator, Tim Browning, explains the need to be familiar with both forms of scale:

> People who understand imperial generally like to think that it is a more human scale, more easily visualized, but it's a matter of what you're used to. The US don't do metric, Europe doesn't do Imperial, the UK is comfortable with both: we draw mainly in imperial, but the suppliers of all the stock materials, timber, steel, mouldings, fittings etc. work in metric, which can be a little confusing.
>
> (Interview with author, 2011)

IMPERIAL MEASURE

This shows base units of measure as well as the ratio of inches to the foot, it can also be shown as x″ = 1′ – 0′. Scales of ¼″ = 1′ and ½″ = 1′, 1″ = 1′ are industry standards, but other increments can be more suitable for specific drafts. Trying to understand imperial measures can be quite daunting if you have only ever worked in metric! However, it is important to get your head around it, and to be able to identify and interpret each scale and its base unit. For example 1″ = 1′ scale means that 1 inch represents 1 foot and is shown as a ratio of 1:12. The easiest way to remember it is by understanding that 12 inches is equivalent to a foot, therefore all base units are divided by 12.

¼″ = 1′ or 12/0.25 = 48	Ratio is 1:48
½″ = 1′ or 12/0.5 = 24	Ratio is 1:24
⅛″ = 1′ or 12/0.0125 = 96	Ratio is 1:96
¾″ = 1′ or 12/0.75 = 16	Ratio is 1:16
1″ = 1′ or 12/1 = 12	Ratio is 1:12
1 ½″ = 1′ or 12/1.5 = 8	Ratio is 1:8

METRIC MEASURE

This differs as scales are only shown as ratios, so the ratio will tell you the scale and its related units of measure. In the UK and across the world the units of measure are in millimetres (mm) and metres (m), with the exception of France where centimetres (cm) and metres (m) are used. A scale of 1:1 means that the 1 before the colon represents an actual centimetre and the number after the colon represents the measurement 1cm will represent. So in this case, 1cm is represented by 1cm as shown on a standard ruler, they are one and the same.

Scale 1:20: In a scale of 1:20, 1 cm = 20cm. This means that 20cm will be represented by 1cm in reality. This would be annotated on drawings as 10mm = 200mm.

Scale 1:25: In a scale of 1:25, 25cm will be represented by 1cm in reality, and noted on drawings as 10mm = 250mm.

Scale 1:50: A scale of 1:50 means that 50cm is represented by 1cm in reality and again will be annotated as 10mm = 500mm. This will be the same for other scales such as 1:100, 1:200 and so on. It is important to remember that 1:250 and 1:2500 are not the same as a 1:25 scale. A 1:250 scale means that 250cm (2.5m) will be represented by a standard 1cm (10mm = 2500mm), and a scale of 1:2500 is 2,500cm (25m) will be represented by a standard 1cm (10mm = 25,000mm).

CURVE SHAPES

These plastic curved templates allow you to draw most universal curves with ease. Template shapes provide a variety of different shapes and sizes that are very useful when time is short. Flexi curves are ideal for measuring round curved objects.

T-SQUARES

T-squares are useful tools that help maintain true horizon lines. They are designed to fit smoothly along the side of a drafting board and smooth enough to run up and down it seamlessly creating true parallel lines. Take care to ensure that it is always flush against the vertical edge of the board to maintain true lines. It is a good idea to buy a T-square that stretches all the way across your drafting media. Choose a larger rather than a smaller one, as this gives you more versatility when drawing on different paper sizes. Take care of this tool, because, if dropped, its right angle can be distorted. Never use it to cut against, as this will deform it, making it useless.

SET SQUARE/ADJUSTABLE SET SQUARE

These transparent plastic triangles can be used on their own, or placed on a T-square or a parallel arm on a drafting board to achieve specific angles. These tools also have bevelled edges that avoid ink smudges. Set squares come in two shapes: 45 degrees and 60 degrees. The 45 degree set square features angles of 90, 45 and 45, whereas the 60 degree set square features 90, 60 and 30 degrees. Adjustable set squares have the added versatility to create any angle and multiple angles.

PROTRACTORS
Mark out degrees with great precision. They come in 180 and 360 degree formats.

BOW COMPASS
Creates circles and arcs, with precision. I recommend you to invest in a decent, robust model that can be adjusted quickly. Consider buying one with extras, such as an extension bar for added versatility.

MASKING TAPE
Ideal for fastening tracing or drafting paper to your drawing board/surface. It is secure and can be removed without damaging the drawing.

PAPER TYPES
Various weights of paper can be used for drafting. Depending on the size of the drawing, drafting paper comes in sheet form or rolls.

DETAIL PAPER
A traditional choice for a draughtsperson, it is a lightweight semi-transparent paper that is a good all rounder that comes in weights of 53gsm or 63gsm.

TRACING OR TRACE PAPER
Semi-transparent, and comes in weights of 60gsm, 90gsm, 116gsm. This paper ages well, however, the lighter weights, 60gsm and 90gsm, have a tendency to crease and tear, and don't react well to moisture. The heavier weight is much more resilient.

DRAFTING FILM
The most stable of all the drawing papers (recommended for dye-line printing). It comes in a variety of weights from 50 to112gsm. It has a smooth matte finish with little distortion or tearing, taking both pencils and inks.

DRAFTING BOARD
Drafting boards are designed for table use. Some varieties are portable (depending on the size), but all have a parallel motion system with a horizontal rule or arm that glides up and down the board smoothly. The angle of the drawing board is limited and can be frustrating. However, it is still a good base to use other drawing equipment, such as setsquares and curves.

DRAFTING TABLE
These have more scope and versatility than drafting boards. Most are height adjustable with flexible boards that can be fixed at any angle, allowing the user to work standing up or sitting down. All provide a parallel motion system allowing smooth movement across the board. These boards can be expensive, but are worth the investment. If your purse does not stretch that far, consider buying a good second hand model online. But make sure that all the components work, otherwise you may as well use a kitchen table!

SURVEYING

An essential part of the interpretation process, it requires deft observation skills and the ability to measure and record information accurately in a clear and logical way. Before designing an environment, it is important to understand the terrain composition and geographical detail/physical make-up of the environment – anything that might impact on what you intend to do with the space, and also what might hamper the shooting process. Accuracy is important, as it can be costly if it's not correct. Freehand drawing is of great value here. Creating proportionally correct drawings can be translated easily into accurate technical drawings (see Figs 94 and 95).

This skill has progressively become more important, as possible shooting environments have increased dramatically. Sets are no longer only built on sound studios, but are built in pre-existing structures or buildings and on exterior locations. Therefore it is very important to understand the environment you intend to build in or on, before considering the set.

A location scout will initially be briefed on what environments need to be found. They should have a comprehensive impression of the space. Sometimes the Production Designer and Art Director will visit possible sites with the Director and DoP to get a feel for the space and whether or not it will suit the scene. Once an environment has been confirmed, a survey of the site must take place. When carrying out a survey, make sure that you are equipped with the right tools for the job. You should have the following:

- Flexible tape measure – 30ft or longer.
- Pencil.
- Pad of layout paper – choose a decent size, such as A3.
- Construction measuring tape or carpenters ruler.
- Most importantly a camera. These days digital will give you better idea of light and quality of the space.

It is crucial to be aware that the survey being carried out is for the production, not only for the art department. Many departments rely on the information recorded. The Director will be interested in how he or she can use the space for action, whereas the DoP will need to determine the quality of light, how much space is available for camera and lighting equipment and position, as well any specific equipment needed.

In Chapter 8 of Tomris Tangaz's book *The Inte-*

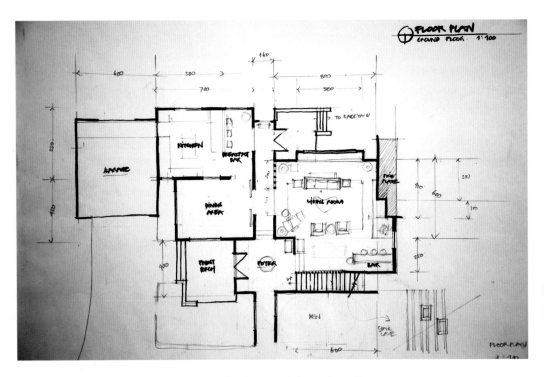

Fig. 94   Freehand technical drawing 1. (Designer: Rini Handayani)

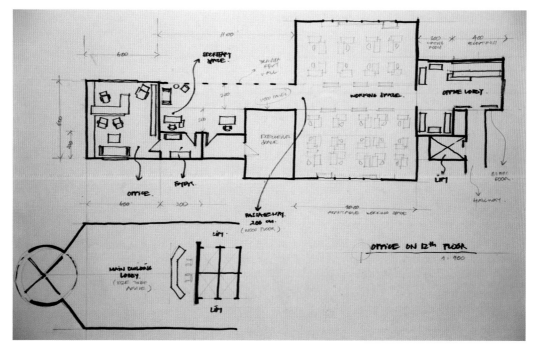

Fig. 95   Freehand technical drawing 2. (Designer: Rini Handayani)

rior: principles, practices and techniques for the aspiring designer, she lays out a very clear and easy to follow method of carrying out a survey. She suggests obtaining pre-existing drawings and photographs. This will provide initial insight into the space. Do note however, that this is not an acceptable substitute for your own survey, as previous surveys may have inaccuracies.

The next stage is to prepare a freehand plan view of the site, so that you can note measurements efficiently and logically. This sketch should be proportionately accurate; Tangaz recommends pacing out the space, noting the architectural shape and elements along the way, such as windows, doors, fireplaces, staircases, radiators, and marking on the plan features that need to be hidden, for example, fuse boxes. When measuring and recording data, try to work with a partner, who will be able to assist by securing the

tape measure and marking down the measurements as you call them out. This is an ideal way to work, but not always possible. If you have to survey an area alone, it is imperative not to rush. Speed can lead to inaccuracy and misinterpretation, so make sure that you work at a comfortable pace.

As the set is temporary, note what you can and can't do with the space and what the owner will let you get away with. Acute observation skills are vital when photo-documenting details. For instance, fixtures and fittings, such as ceiling roses, lights, electrical sockets, door knobs and so on, types of building materials and their construction, such as floorboards, beams, staircases, balustrade and so on and their characteristics, that is, colour, texture, style, form, mouldings and so on and their condition.

Exterior location shoots require surveying, especially if additions are being made to structures or if structures are being placed in or on a location.

When surveying an exterior location, record geographic observations. What are the contours and characteristics of the terrain and the quality of it? Is it stable? What is the composition? What area mass will be built upon? Will the ground structure support a near life-sized set? Will is look good on camera? And so on.

Draughtsman and Illustrator, Tim Browning, explains the process when building Kate Winslet's cottage in *The Holiday* (2006) on location:

> The location scouts scoured the country for the perfect cottage. There were a few good looking options but they were all impractical. Shooting on distant location comes with many and various costs and it will often be cheaper to just build the set somewhere closer to home. That way you also get to design the set exactly the way you want, once you've found the right field, with enough space nearby for the unit to set up a base and park its trucks. For this cottage we needed to level a small patch of ground by digging into the hillside, we removed a few established plants, and planted others, some real, some fake, we laid temporary roadway between the unit base and the set, we carved paths and roads into the field as part of the set. Aesthetically the choice of location will inevitably influence the design of the set.
>
> (Interview with author, 2011)

Photos are as fundamental as the measurements, so make that you are comfortable with your camera. Common sense is of the essence here, as each picture is a representation. Avoid artistic and abstract shots – these are for documenting, so make sure there is adequate light. Because of the 3-D nature of objects and space, take shots from different angles. If you are not the person drawing up the plans, your draughtsperson will be most grateful. A Polaroid camera captures images quickly, but can be expensive. Digital cameras can capture the quality of light and accurately represent objects and space. In addition to stills capture, use a video camera to walk the space, recording the feel and sense of space. A video camera is essential when surveying an exterior environment for tangibility. It provides scale and geographic form, which can be distorted on stills.

Prior to conducting a survey, it is worth making a few notes on what the space will be used for. This will help you to focus on the data that needs to be collected and put it into context. As an assistant, anticipation is a core skill to have. Through working with Designers, an assistant should instinctively know what they need from a space in addition to the basic area survey. In the early stages of a working relationship, do not be afraid to ask your Designer for guidance. Never assume, always check to confirm requirements beforehand.

ALLOWANCES

Providing adequate space for the camera, lighting equipment and crew to work carefully and efficiently around a set is vital. Allowances should also be considered in order for the set and scenic backdrops to be lit in a way that appears convincing on screen. Tim Browning explains:

> The stage layout is a key discipline which must account for unit access, fire lanes and appropriate distance between set and scenic backing. A painted or printed backing can generally sit approximately 25' from the set, and a *translite* (a back-lit printed photograph) will need 15' behind it for lighting. Enough distance must be provided for the backing to be lit effectively to achieve a believable level of authenticity. All set specific issues need to be discussed with the Gaffer, and anyone else involved. For example, if sections of a set need to come away (wild or floating walls) to capture a specific shot,

Task 4: Practise Surveying

Using the step-by-step process in the section above, carry out a survey for an interior (your flat or a floor of your house for example) and an exterior space (a garden, for example). Create a freehand drawing, complete with detailed form, measurements with supporting photographic documentation.

Up for more of challenge? Survey your space in different measuring formats – imperial and metric.

Task 5: Create a Plan View

Using the information from the previous task, draw a plan view with elevations of the space. Show all perimeter lines as single clad walls, and interior walls as double-cladded.

For more of a challenge, draft one in imperial (¼″) and the other in metric (1:25). Depending on the size of the area you are surveying, scale your drawing to the size of the paper.

you need to discuss the logistics of the shot. When a set occupies most of all the free space on the stage, it can be difficult, but not impossible for the unit to work around it. The advantages and disadvantages should always be discussed with all key parties prior to set up. The majority of set designs will naturally leave enough dead space around them for the shooting crew to make themselves comfortable and set up their various bases.

(Interview with the author, 2011)

COMPUTER SKILLS

Designers have embraced 3-D modelling software for stage and screen alike. These programs mean that all drawings maintain a consistent look, neatness and readability. Some people argue that there is no real individualism between draughtspeople apart from the lettering. However the advantages are that the drafting language becomes universal, and can minimize the time taken to hand draft, and important artistic flourishes can be applied in graphic design programs. Errors can be revised with ease, whereas errors on hand drawings may need to be redrawn from scratch, not ideal if it's taken two to three hours to create – saving time and elevated blood pressure.

Programs that have cross-platform capabilities provide a seamless transition from 2-D drawings into 3-D. The advantages of working in an electronic format means that plans can be emailed to the construction team without laboriously translating endless drawings. Another advantage is it allows the draughtsperson the opportunity to see the set from any angle, through various lenses, at any given time to make sure that it works. It captures lens projections that would otherwise be extremely time consuming and tedious to achieve by hand. Varying versions have set design, lighting and scenery capabilities.

Make sure that you research all the versions and find the best that works for you. Find out what you country's industry standard is. Many Production Designers now prefer their draughtspeople to produce drawings very quickly. Most draughtspeople in the industry are capable of producing hand drawn and computer drafts.

With pre-production times becoming ever shorter it is an ideal tool that cuts down drafting time, and gets all the relevant plans out as soon as possible.

7 Model-Making: the Basics

WHY DO WE NEED MODELS?

Models are the next step in the realization of your design. Model making is an important skill for anyone wanting a career in any of the screen design industries. It is a medium that is used in many forms. From sketch to detailed models to miniature sets used for filming: like animation, model making allows the designer complete understanding of their design and it is also a way to ensure that all works well before life-sized construction commences.

At a time when screen design became more digital age, model-making skills were being replaced by CGI (Computer Generated Imagery) programs. However, recently there has been a resurgence in the art of model making. This skill is more relevant in today's industries; it bridges the gap between 2-D conceptualization and 3-D realization. Production Designer Eve Stewart supports the need for models:

A model is still essential. Many directors and producers do not understand scale and you cannot plan for shots other than those realized in the computer visuals unless you can see the sets in all their dimensions in advance.

(Interview with author, 2011)

OPPOSITE: **Fig. 96** **Model made by the author.**

Models for film, television and video are generally less detailed than the versions used by theatre designers and architects. Screen models were born out of theatrical and architectural models where vast detail is applied. Theatrical models have always been an essential tool for showing a production's detail and mechanics. The Designer is not only presenting ideas and design, but also offering strategies to magically tell a story in front of a live audience – something which is not of the utmost importance for a Screen Designer. Architectural models work in a similar detailed way, where special focus is placed on the design and complex structural engineering. This differs from their screen counterparts, which represent structures and surfaces that are only important in achieving the captured image. However, this is not always the case; the level of detail depends on the purpose of the model. Models that are intended for filming are highly detailed, as they have to resemble their life-sized equivalents to fit in a pre-existing landscape. Models also help to understand space, they add the extra dimension to a set and allow the designer and crew to visualize, identify and rectify problems that could prove costly if ignored.

DESIGNING IN 3-D

It is not enough to create a 3-D design in 2-D and start construction. Creating a 3-D model allows you to check that things work before construction. There will always be adjustments and changes during construction, but preparation is extremely important. Models are not just pretty miniature sets; they allow the Designer time to work through logistical challenges, such as budget constraints, architectural details and how the camera captures action in the created environment. The Designer must never forget that performers, crew and equipment work in the space and should make allowances accordingly (*see* Chapter 6).

Personally, I like to work on technical drawings with the model at the same time, allowing a total understanding of the vision. By putting ideas into the model, you get a real sense of objects in space. Working through objects in space in 2-D can be distorting. Rarely do the images in our heads translate perfectly first time. That is why this process is so vital. When starting out in the industry it is important to find out what is the best way of working for you. You will have little time to do this once you start work, because of the fast paced nature of the work. During pre-production, crew members are expected to hit the ground running, so proficiency in skills such as 3-D model making is important. Of course, some Designers don't work

with models. They aren't always necessary or even possible; but it is amazing how transferable this skill is. Different models fulfil different functions. Below is a description of a variety of models used in screen design and their functions.

ILLUSTRATIVE OR SKETCH

Used for preliminary ideas. Give the designer the chance to explore texture, colour and form in space. They are much rougher, not necessarily to scale, use broader strokes, making them much more artistically powerful.

DESIGN OR CONCEPTUAL

This model type brings design and correct scale knowledge together, incorporating texture, colour and form to develop the design (*see* Fig. 97). These are usually used as the communication tool for conceptualization process during pre-production.

TECHNICAL/BLUE PRINT/DYE LINE

These are more accurate in scale and dimensions (Fig. 98). Dye line and blue print copies produce

Fig. 97 Design/ conceptual model with textures. (Designer: Marielle Misson Pereira)

Fig. 98 Technical model, where drafting plans are attached to the foam board surface.

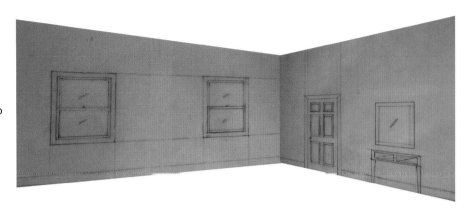

technically correct scaled plans. Photocopies are never as accurate, as they distort the dimensions when printed. Colour and texture are not applied, as it is purely to illustrate precise dimension and construction in scale.

MODELS FOR CAMERA CAPTURE

These combine design and technical details. This model is for filming; therefore the concept, craftsmanship, detail and scale have to be perfect, as it will be the basis for the captured image. This model can also be used for initial filming and then manipulated in post-production. Some are constructed with form, in a neutral colour, so that digital rendering can be applied en masse. Or it can be used in stop motion animation, such as Aardman's *Wallace and Gromit*.

TOOLS FOR THE JOB

When embarking on a model making project it is most important to choose the correct materials and equipment for the job. Some argue that this starves one's creativity, but when it comes to working in scale there will always be some type of creative challenge. Don't forget, this model, along with technical drawings, is the beginning of 3-D realization, therefore the Designer and the design team

have a duty to produce an accurate representation so that all can visualize the end product.

RAW MATERIALS

Most models are made from lightweight materials that maintain structure and form. Rarely does a model stay in one place, so it has to be made out of durable materials and well constructed. Foam board or poly board is a popular choice for most structural construction. Each sheet consists of a plastic foam centre (*see* Fig. 99), sandwiched between two thin layers of paper.

Foam board is available in various thicknesses: 3mm, 5mm, and 10mm, and comes in various neutral colours: full white with a slight gloss finish; full black matte; white foam sandwiched between

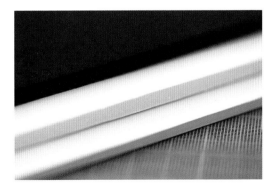

Fig. 99   Varieties of foam board/poly board.

black matte paper and white foam sandwiched between grey matte paper. The full black foam board is very popular with theatre designers, as it closely represents their environment, however, it is also the most expensive. So, if you are on a limited budget, choose full white. It will mean that you have more white to cover up, but it will save money. It is also helpful to know that the thicker this product gets, the dearer it is, so take this into account when choosing material.

Even though foam board is sturdy, it can also be fragile. As paper and foam are porous materials, it absorbs moisture quickly and begins to warp. Once distorted, it is difficult to force it back into its original state. The thinner the board, the more delicate it is. It should be carefully stored in a dry place, away from central heating, as it does not react well to moisture or heat. When used for miniature and animation work, it needs to be sealed properly so that the heat from studio lights doesn't warp the material.

MOUNT BOARD AND OTHER CARDS

The use of mount board (2mm thick card used for framing borders) and varying thicknesses of card are good companions for foam board. The thinner the card the more flexibility it has to create curves and shapes for working to scale. These also are good materials for intricate details and features, such as door and window frames, skirting boards and staircases.

EQUIPMENT AND TOOLS

Scale models for the screen need to be accurate. Before beginning, make sure that you have an adequate sized work surface that is level and well lit. You also need a comfortable chair. Below is a list of basic equipment and tools that every model maker should have in their toolbox.

CUTTING MAT

A cutting mat provides a level surface on which to cut materials as precisely as possible. Choose a self-healing cutting mat, as they are longer lasting and more resilient. They come in a range of sizes from A4 to A0. It is a good idea to purchase a large cutting mat, as this will not limit the size in which you can work.

METRIC AND IMPERIAL RULERS

Multi-scale rulers are vital for model making. They maintain the scale ratio during the drafting and making process. They come in prism shapes, with multiple scale ratios. Always double-check that you are using the correct scale, it is easy to get muddled. These rulers should be used only to measure, and never to cut against.

METAL RULERS

Used for measuring on a 1:1 ratio scale, and are much more resilient than their wooden and plastic counterparts. More importantly, they can be used for cutting against. However, metal rulers are smooth surfaced and can slip and slide, resulting in inaccurate cutting and possible injury. Some have a cork strip along one side to prevent movement. If these aren't available, apply a strip of masking tape to the underside of an ordinary metal ruler, which should do the job. The best rulers for cutting are grooved rulers, which are especially designed for this purpose. They are safer and more stable when using craft knives and scalpels – position the fingers in the groove helps to avoid fingers coming into contact with sharp blades. You can get them in most good art supplies shops.

It is good practice to have a variety of different-sized rulers for precision cutting.

TRANSPARENT ACRYLIC RULERS

Have measured increments of 5mm to 50mm, so that it makes it easier to cut evenly with speed. They also have metal edges, making them ideal for cutting against. Remember to only use metal straight edges for cutting. Sharp blades will cut into plastic and wood edges rendering them useless.

T-SQUARE, SET SQUARE AND PROTRACTORS
Have the same uses as with technical drawing. They help create precise straight edges and correct degree angles which are crucial in model making construction.

FRENCH CURVES
Used to create dimensionally correct, consistent curves, when free hand drawing is not accurate enough.

CUTTING BLADES
Craft knives and scalpels cut all forms of card, foam board, paper, and thin plastics, such as acrylic and Perspex. Craft knives come in two sizes and have safety features. Before using this tool, make sure that you know how to use it safely. Craft knives have grooves down the blade, so that when the blade becomes blunt, it can be snapped off. Do this with the help of the attachment at the base of the knife. You may find a small pair of pliers will offer more purchase – but whichever way you decide to break the blade, do it with care.

Scalpels are much sharper, and have no safety mechanism; so take more care when using this tool, which will cut through flesh! Make sure that you always cut with a sharp blade and that you always have a good supply of them. When changing scalpel blades, use both your thumbs and forefingers to gently lift the bottom of the blade up and carefully slide it off. To fit a new one, simply fit the blade onto the groove of the handle and press the tip of the blade down on a cutting mat

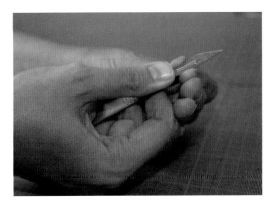

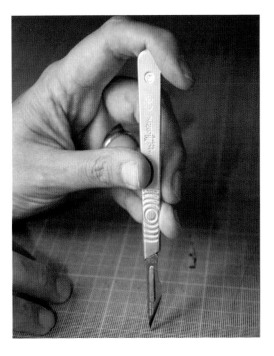

TOP: Fig. 100   Removing scalpel blade.
MIDDLE: Fig. 101   Replacing a scalpel blade.
BOTTOM: Fig. 102   Press blade into mat to secure it.

to secure it (*see* Figs 100 to 102). Do not press the blade on any other work surface, as it will become blunt before you even begin. Dispose of blunt blades safely, by folding them in paper.

ADHESIVE TAPE

Used for temporary and permanent fixing. Double-sided tape is used when glue would be too messy. It is used a lot in presentation models, as it gives a clean, professional finish. Masking tape is a temporary fixing tape, and as the name suggests, it also masks areas to achieve precise paint applications and finishing. Gum strip becomes adhesive when wet. It is used to cover uneven surfaces and dries quickly – it is similar to papier maché, without the mess.

GLUES

Choosing the appropriate adhesive for the job is very important. As previously mentioned, not all glues react positively or are effective with certain materials. For example, multi-purpose liquid glues eat away the plastic foam in foam board, leaving only an ugly brittle shell. When attaching foam edges, always use water-based glues, such as PVA or wood glues. The glues are strong and dry to a transparent finish. Do not use these types of glue on the foam board's paper surfaces, as they will absorb the water and warp the material. Multi-purpose glues are versatile and can be used to glue most fabrics, card and paper. On thinner paper, choose a stick glue rather than a liquid, to avoid bubbling. For more specific materials, such as plastics, metals, ceramics and wood, choose specific glues for the task.

Visit your local model shop or art supplies shop for guidance, they should have a good variety. Spray glue is particularly good for model making. It can be applied lightly and evenly, leaving smooth surfaces, especially on foam board because it does not warp. Spray evenly and to the edges to avoid edges lifting off. Only use this glue in a well-ventilated area and preferably in a spray booth, as glue particles can be harmful when inhaled.

Liquid glues that are not water-based, such spray, super, and solvent specific, can be highly toxic and irritate the skin, as well as bond it in seconds, so be very careful when using them and always read the labels.

OTHER TOOLS

Flat-headed dressmaking pins are ideal for pinning foam board together. They are especially useful in the early stages of conceptualization and construction. Pins allow flexibility when adjusting and transporting the model to preserve it. They are also useful for keeping things together and keeping things in place while they dry.

Model-making tweezers are a must for the toolbox. The long pointed ends are extremely useful when placing objects in hard-to-reach places.

Mechanical pencils are used for drafting and marking. Always use an H or HB lead weight, to avoid loss of valuable millimetres when mapping out sections.

MATERIALS

WOOD

Using wood in scale models is not always effective and practical. Balsa wood is lightweight, without an obvious grain, making it ideal for covering surface areas. Thin wood veneers with fine grains can be used to create wall panelling and floorboards. These types of wood react well to wood staining solutions, giving an authentic look with ease.

PLASTICS

There is a huge variety of plastics and acrylics on offer for model making. They come in varying thicknesses of sheets, hollow tubes and solid rods, and are very effective in representing glass and plastic. Plastics can be sourced from specialist model shops and plastics suppliers. Depending on the thickness, it can be cut, heated and moulded, or vacuum formed to create specific shapes and objects. And it is particularly effective when experimenting with lighting states. Introducing light can create an illuminating or neon effect.

FABRIC

Fabrics can add realism to a scale model, but can also break the scale. Fabric is at a 1:1 scale, therefore a heavy jute hessian, for example, will be out of scale once placed in the model. This is because it represents something much larger in reality. Choosing smoother fabrics rather than highly textured ones may feel a little dull, but never forget that the design needs to be in scale. Challenge yourself to find other alternatives that capture the textural quality in scale. Think carefully before using printed fabrics for the same reason. In some instances it is more effective to use scaled down prints as an alternative (see Chapter 8). Try measuring the desired print, and then converting it to the model's scale, to see how much you need to reduce it. Through practice and application, you will find out which materials work better, and how best to illustrate them in a scaled environment.

Do's and Don'ts when Working with Foam Board

Do:
- Cut foam board with a very sharp blade and on a cutting mat.
- Use water-based glues, such as PVA and wood glue, when sticking foam edges.
- Choose multi-purpose liquid, stick and spray glues for paper surfaces.
- Paint colour on a separate material and then attach it with spray, stick or multi-purpose glue to avoid warping.

Don't:
- Use multi-purpose glues to glue foam edges. They will corrode the foam.
- Apply paint, especially water-based, directly to the paper surface, as it will absorb the moisture and warp.
- Store material in heated or damp conditions, even when constructed, it will still warp.

Task 1: Constructing a Basic White Shell

1. Begin by studying the technical drawings, making sure that you understand the basic structure and how the components will be attached (see Fig. 103).
2. Select a thickness of foam board. For this task, use 5mm white board. 3mm or 5mm are both ideal for creating a model's walls and floor. The thicker versions are not so flexible for scaled work, but can be used as a sturdy base on which to mount the finished model.

Fig. 103   Translate measurements to foam board.

Fig. 104   Add adequate allowance.

3. When mapping out each segment, it is vital to include model construction allowances. Without these, the model will lose space. Think twice if the model is 10mm smaller than intended, because this could actually mean a loss of 20cm on a 1:25 scale, or as much as 100cm in scale of 1:100. Before adding any allowances, decide on the floor. Will the model be constructed on a larger base, or will it be the exact dimensions of the room itself? It may be beneficial to include space around the model, especially if the set is built in a studio space (like the interior of a house, or a set for a television game show, for example), or set in a very specific terrain on location.

4. Once you've decided, begin drafting out the floor. If you have opted for on a larger base, be sure to centre it, so that people are not fixated on the position of the model, rather than the model itself. If the base is the size of the room, add an allowance around the entire perimeter. The allowance should correspond to the thickness of the foam board (see Fig. 104). In this case, it will be 5mm. Alternatively, you can choose not to add any perimeter allowances, but remember, you will need to compensate by adding allowance to the walls.

5. Now begin to roughly map out the pieces needed for the model. There should be five pieces in all: four walls and one floor. Try to use each sheet economically by arranging paper templates. If you feel confident, draft the dimensions straight onto the foam board with a mechanical pencil. Remember, the measurements and angles at this stage need to be correct. Double-check everything with a ruler or setsquare before making the first cut. Apply puncture points by laying the technical drawing on top of the foam board.

6. Once the floor has been drafted and allowances added, carefully cut out the base with a sharp scalpel and label it A.

7. Now map out the walls. Draft the walls that are same dimensions. In this task they will be the opposite walls. Remember to add 5mm allowances. Both horizontal sides of the wall must have assembling allowances. Depending on how you have chosen to construct the

model, add allowances accordingly. If the model base is bigger than the room, do not add allowance to the height of the walls. If the model's base has had allowances added, again, there is no need to add additional allowance. However, if the floor base has no allowance added, you need to add a 5mm allowance to the height of the walls.

8. Once a wall has been correctly drafted, repeat the process with the opposite wall. As this room is an even cube shape, the opposite wall will have identical dimensions. Cut out both of these pieces and label them B and C.

9. Carry on and draft the two remaining walls. This time, only adding allowance to the height, as the base has had no allowance added. Note that allowance is not added to the wall width, as each will be attached to the allowance given to walls B and C. Cut out the wall pieces and label them D and E. Note: allowances can be added to either set of walls. Choose opposite walls to avoid confusion. This method can be followed with any shaped environment, as the principles are the same.

10. If there are any features, such as windows and a door, in this case, draft and cut them out before construction. Again, depending on your method of assembly, if the walls have an allowance added to the height, remember to mark out the doors and windows from the allowance point, not from the bottom edge of the wall. Measuring these features from the bottom edge will lose valuable height, foreshortening the doorway and window placements.

11. Arrange pieces as in Fig. 105. Now you are ready to construct. Make sure that you have flat-headed pins to hand.

12. Begin attaching pieces B and D. Pin the walls together along wall B's allowance (*see* Fig. 106). Avoid using lots of pins, when two or three will do. Repeat the same process with walls C and E.

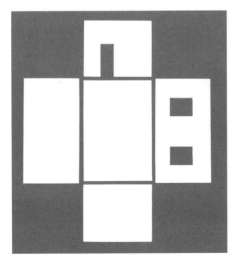

Fig. 105   Lay out the pieces in the way they will be attached.

Fig. 106   Pin wall to the floor with long flat pins.

LEFT: **Fig. 107   Attaching the walls.**

TOP: **Fig. 108   The finished white shell model.**

13. If the floor has no allowances added, attach the walls to the floor by pushing pins along the wall base edges to secure them together (see Fig. 107). If the floor does have allowance added, push pins from the underside, so that they sit vertically upright. Then press each pair of walls down onto the pins, so that the walls and floor are now attached.

14. To finish, pin the remaining walls together.

Alternatively you can glue the base of the model together, but this depends on the purpose of the model. Gluing the model together sets it in one state, and this may not be useful in discussions, when you want to remove walls and look at the set from different camera angles as part of the design process.

During the development stage, the model should be easily manipulable to accommodate any pre-production changes. This method can be followed when making a dye-line or blue print model. Instead of plotting the dimensions on the foam board, spray glue a copy of the plans directly onto the board, and then follow the steps for adding allowance through to assembling.

USEFUL MODEL-MAKING TECHNIQUES

The following techniques offer simple ways to achieve certain shapes and structures; they are by no means the only way to do things. Through experimentation and practice you will find your own methods.

JOINS

Task 1 describes a fast, effective way to create a model with exposed foam joins. This is adequate for rough sketch models. However, when the purpose of the model demands a higher level of detail and quality, you should use hidden joins.

This technique is ideal for foam board. Begin with two walls. One wall will have the added allowance (that is, the thickness of the foam board). Make sure that the measurements are exactly the same on both ends. Connect the ends with a straight line, making sure that it is perpendicular. Carefully, with a metal ruler and a sharp bladed scalpel, gently pierce the top layer of paper and cut across (Fig. 109). Gradually apply a little more pressure to cut through the foam, but not through the paper layer on the other side.

Gently run the flat side of the scalpel blade along the paper edge to release the foam column (Fig. 110). For the best quality join, try to get as close to the paper as possible. Once the excess foam board is removed, spread a small amount of PVA or wood glue into the groove (Fig. 111). Then join the two walls, removing any excess glue. Carefully place the joined walls on an even surface till completely dry (Fig. 112). This technique produces attractive, clean and strong joins.

Fig. 109   Hidden join – carefully cutting through foam middle.

Fig. 110   Remove the section of foam.

Fig. 111   Apply water-based glue, such as PVA, to the groove.

Fig. 112   Secure pieces, then leave to dry.

CREATING ASYMMETRICAL WALLED ENVIRONMENTS

With architectural forms being used more and more in all forms of screen design, model makers are constantly under pressure to create these features in miniature. Asymmetrical environments can be easily achieved using foam board.

The simplest method is to begin with the floor plan, which dictates the shape of the room. Measure the perimeter of the room, applying assembling allowance to one side. Mark the corner points in which the walls change angle, and using a set square, extend perpendicular lines upwards. Then carefully, from the other side, using a metal ruler and a scalpel, cut through the outer layer of paper and down though the layer of foam, without piercing the other paper layer.

Continue to cut all the corners in the same way. Carefully, begin to fold the joins inwards to create the angled walls, and either pin or glue them in place.

CREATING CURVES

Curved shapes can be created using mount board, card, foam board and heavyweight paper. The latter is the easiest to manipulate but not particularly sturdy; it is best suited to curved details, such as cycloramas. Foam board, mount board and card are used to create sturdier structures such as walls. Begin by marking out a series of perpendicular lines of equal spacing in the opposite direction of the intended curve.

Using a scalpel blade and metal ruler, gently cut through the top layer of paper and foam layer only (Fig. 113). Cut through the series of lines, making sure that all incisions are the same depth. At this point, you will be able to feel the flexibility and can create the curve according to the design specifications (Fig. 114). Once the curve is established, it can be fixed to the floor with either pins or glue (Fig. 115). When creating a curved feature with mount board or card, mark out the same series

Fig. 113   Scoring foam board for a curved wall.

Fig. 114   Gently bend the wall to create the shape.

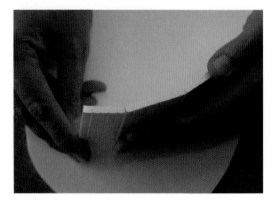

Fig. 115   Position of base and pin.

of lines equidistant apart. Depending on the thickness of the material, either run the scalpel blade along, scoring each line gently to avoid cutting right though. If the card/board is thin (approximately 2mm), use the back of the blade to score the lines. Once scoring is complete, the board/card will be more pliable and can be fastened in the same way as before.

OTHER 3 D SHAPES

A dome is particularly difficult to achieve with perfect symmetry in card and paper. When there is little time, it's best not to construct complex shapes. Instead, visit your local model shop for alternatives, or create them from a mould in fibreglass resin, or vacuum-formed plastic or with gum strip.

COLUMNS AND PILLARS

Depending on its cross-section, pillars or columns can be created with tubing or wooden dowel for cylindrical pillars and foam board or mount board for oblong shapes. Experiment with various materials to get the look you want.

CREATING A STAIRCASE

To construct a staircase, use mount board rather than foam board. Mount board is thick and sturdy enough to maintain scale. Choose a 2mm thickness for the sides of the staircase. Trace a copy from the technical drawing and with a soft leaded pencil, colour in the outline on the back. Use strips of masking tape to hold the tracing paper in place and with a ruler and mechanical pencil, draw the outline of the staircase twice, and cut both out (Fig. 116). Measure the width of the staircase and cut a base and vertical support. Glue both sides of the staircase to the base and to the vertical support. To make sure that the dimensions remain constant, insert another strip of card of the same width in between for a solid shape. Now cut out enough tread strips and riser strips to cover

Fig. 116 The staircase is calculated by the depth and height of each step.

the staircase out of a 1mm card. Applying a thin layer of PVA or multi-purpose glue to the edges, attach all the risers, and then all the tread. You may find that model tweezers come in handy when positioning each strip (Fig. 117). This method can be used for curved, sweeping and uneven stairways.

Fig. 117   Use tweezers to glue the steps.

Tips and Tricks of Cutting

- When cutting foam board, score gently, then gradually apply more pressure until the blade reaches the cutting mat.
- Never cut on uneven surfaces.
- Always use a sharp blade.

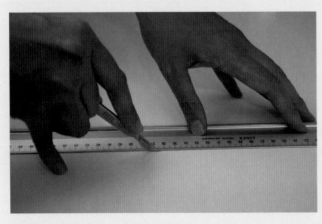

Fig. 118   Keep fingers in the centre groove of the ruler to avoid injury.

- Make sure you use the correct cutting tool – scalpels should be used to cut board of 5mm or less. A craft knife should be used for anything thicker than 5mm.
- Keep your fingers clear of the scalpel blade (*see* Figure 118).
- For accuracy, always stand up when cutting.
- Always cut diagonally away from you (Fig. 119).
- If the foam board has warped, try painting the other side of the board. Alternatively, weigh down the board, by placing it warp-side up, and place some heavy books on top overnight. If this doesn't work, you will have to start again.
- Finally, take your time and concentrate!

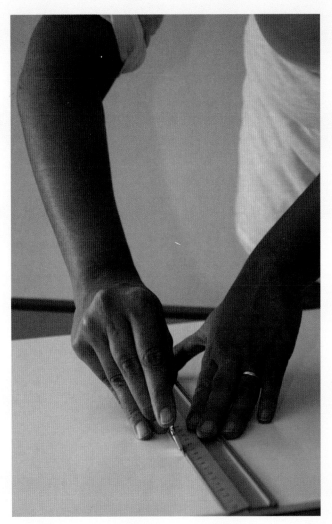

Fig. 119   Always cut away from you.

8 More Detailed Model-Making

FROM WHITE CUT-OUT TO FULLY RENDERED

In the previous chapter we looked at basic models. The next step is to be able to realize more complex shapes and details, in keeping with the design intentions. Whether its purpose is to present the space in terms of spatial composition or to capture the character and feel, a model is a realization tool that bridges a gap between technical drawing and an actual build.

Screen models differ from their stage counter-parts. The traditional screen model is white, or one that has a dye-line print of the technical draft glued onto the surface of the foam board as the only aesthetic feature. However, given the vast range of design requirements for film, television and video projects today, the more versatile and skilled a model maker, the more possibilities they will have in any art department.

Some Designers argue that the age of model making by hand is coming to an end because of computer programs, such as Vectorworks and SketchUp. Time is a luxury that many projects have very little of, and for them the computer has provided a very practical solution. For others, the need to be able to see, touch and feel their way around a model outweighs the practicalities of 3-D

environments on screen. In fact there is space for both practices, assuring an extended life for model makers.

Model makers should understand what type of model is required and be able to meet deadlines. In addition, they must understand the project's language, its context and have an eye for detail to capture that context visually.

Every model maker will have a preferred way of approaching a model. The step-by-step guides below provide simple and easy methods to create a variety of the most common details on any set. Through experimenting with these techniques, you will discover which methods are most comfortable for you and that give the best results.

Before beginning, there a few things to keep in mind. Firstly, never discard any cut out pieces of windows, doors and so on, they will always be useful. Secondly, with all intricate work choose a sharp bladed scalpel rather than a craft knife, for precision cutting. The following features can be used as a basis for all forms of models, depending on the detail required.

FEATURES

DOORS

Doors can be the simplest of all features to construct. There are many variations from glaze, flush, flush and glaze, panelled, sliding to swing doors. All of the above can essentially be formed using the following basic method (Fig. 121).

OPPOSITE: Fig. 120 Model made by the author.

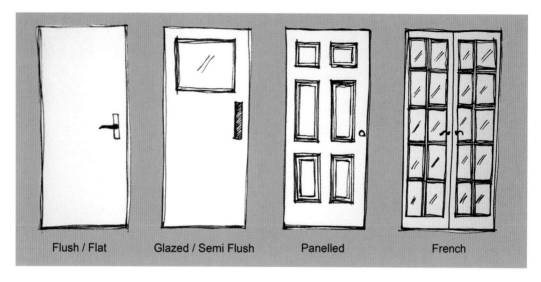

Fig. 121   Types of doors.

FLUSH

A flush door has no surface features, it is smooth and flat with a door handle, and sometimes has a kick plate at the bottom. Depending on the thickness of the poly/foam board used, you can either use the removed cut-out shape, or measure and re-cut another door to the same dimensions as the door frame in a more suitable material, something like thinner poly/foam board, balsa wood, or mount board. Now the door is ready to paint. Decide how you will apply colour keeping in mind what effect certain paint media will have on card and foam board (see Chapter 7).

FLUSH AND GLAZE

This type of door has at least a single pane of glass inset in the door. It is best to select a card that is half the thickness of the door. You will also need a sheet of clear acetate. Begin by measuring out the door's dimensions (Fig. 122), marking in the glass placement (at this stage do not cut out the doors, keep them as part of a larger piece).

Now repeat the previous step, creating a door with exactly the same dimensions. Using a scalpel,

carefully create a right angle incision point in each corner of the glass pane frame (Fig. 123). This will help guide the blade. With a metal ruler, slowly cut through the lines beginning and ending at each incision point, trying not to cut past the point.

Repeat this for the next three sides. The section of card should come away. If not, run the scalpel blade around the frame to release it. Follow the same process with the duplicate door. Once both windows have been removed, cut out the doors carefully. This can be done before, but it is up to you the model maker to decide how confident you are with a scalpel.

For beginners, it is better to keep the doors in a single piece, when the cutting out is intricate. Before beginning construction consider how the door will be attached to its frame, as this will determine how you will create it. Lay a piece of clear acetate over the cut-out window (Fig. 124), and mark out the section with 2 to 3mm allowance around the edges with a fine tipped pen (0.1 or 0.2mm). Cut the acetate out with a sharp pair of scissors or a scalpel, and using either stick or liquid multi-purpose glue, sparingly, apply a thick

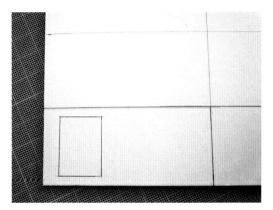

Fig. 122 Mark out the window placement.

Fig. 123 Using a scalpel, make small incisions into the corners for precision cutting.

Fig. 124 Apply acetate to the inside of one door.

line around the perimeter of the window frame. With care, place the acetate on top of the frame, positioning it within the allowance lines on the wrong side of one of the doors. Attach a fabric or paper hinge at this stage. Apply a thin layer of multi-purpose glue onto the same side of the door avoiding the acetate window. Then place the identical door on top and press firmly together. Quickly remove any seepage of glue.

Note: if you intend to add colour and texture to the door, do this before gluing the two sides together.

Task 1: Make a Six-Panelled Door

A panelled door has a raised surface, and like all modern and period versions, comes in a number of designs. The following method is for a typical six panel British Victorian door, but can be adapted to any shape and design. The best way to construct a panelled door is to opt for thinner card; 1 or 2mm thick, which can be glued in layers to achieve the thickness and panel relief. Essentially, this door will be made up of six layers.

Begin by measuring out the door's dimension including the panels within. For this task, use the dimensions featured in Fig. 125. Cut out two identical pieces of Door 1 and set aside as section A and B respectively. Using the same dimensions as Door 1, mark up the panel details within to create Door 2. Mark up two of these pieces and label them A and B lightly in pencil.

Mark each corner point with a corner incision, and carefully cut each panel out and set aside for use as the insets (Fig. 126). Trim each panel cut-out so that it sits within its respective frame in Door 2, section A.

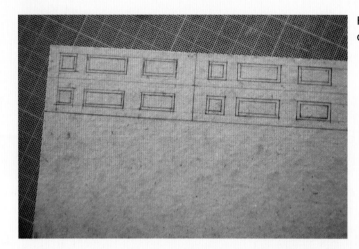

Fig. 125   Draft out door panels twice.

Repeat the same process with Door 2, section B and put aside with all section B pieces (Fig. 127). Take group A (1, 2, 3) pieces, spread a layer of glue to the wrong side of part 2, and place it on top of the right side of part 1. Apply glue and centre each panel in its panel frame. You may find it easier to mark out the panel positions on part 1 lightly with pencil to achieve precise positions.

Set aside, and continue with section B, repeating the same steps as described for section A. For the hinge, insert either a fabric or paper strip to the underside of section A or B's hinge end, then glue the two parts together and leave to dry. Once dry, it is ready to be painted and attached to the wall (Fig. 128). Drawing or inking in the detail with a fine nibbed drawing pen can easily create doors with 2-D panel detail.

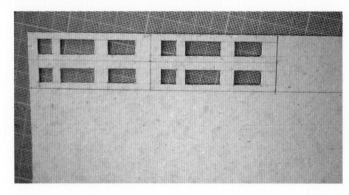

Fig. 126   Cut out the panels before cutting the doors out.

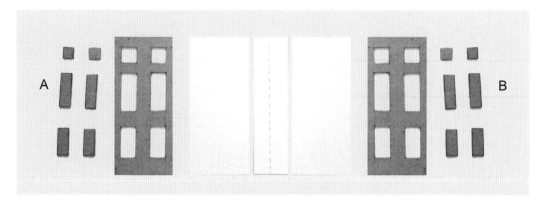

Figs 127 and 128   Place them in groups A and B.

DOOR FURNITURE

Doorknobs, handles and knockers can be made of epoxy modelling putty or wire. Depending on the size and style of the detail, choose the most suitable material. Doorknobs are easily shaped with putty, where as handles are much more achievable with wire. In more elaborate cases a detail can be fashioned with wire to create the structure, and then built up with putty. Other details such as escutcheons and letterboxes can be made using thin 1mm or 2mm card.

Depending on the functionality of the model, functioning doors may be useful so that the Director, Production Designer and the DoP can get down and experience the model at eye level.

HINGES

Hinges can be applied to fulfil a simple action.

Cut a piece of fabric or paper to the height of the door and 20mm or 1 inch wide. Glue half the strip to the underside of the door, leaving the other half free. Then glue the other side of the door on top, sandwiching the strip in between. The loose end can then be glued to the wall. Do this before adding any wall surface treatments such as wallpaper and doorframes. This technique is best for doors that are made up of layers of card.

If the door is a single piece of card or poly/foam board, a piece of paper can be added to the outer side and then covered up with paper. Alternatively, a pivot hinge may be more practical. Feed a thin piece of wire right through the door then fasten securely through the floor and doorframe.

Task 2: Create Windows

Like doors, windows come in many different shapes, styles and sizes, from sash, single pane, multi-pane, double-glazed to stained glass. The technical drawings will give you all the information on design, dimension, and how they sit within the wall – a recess for example. Whatever the shape and style, a window will always have a frame that holds in the panes of glass. As in the previous tasks, select suitable materials.

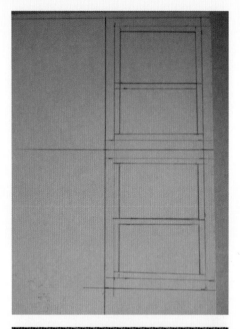

TOP LEFT: Fig. 129   Panelled door in situ.

TOP RIGHT: Fig. 130   Draft of a sash window.

BOTTOM LEFT: Fig. 131   Cut out the centre before cutting out the window.

BOTTOM RIGHT: Fig. 132   Thin card is used to add more depth and detail.

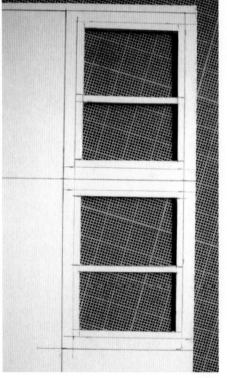

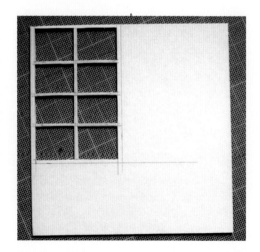

For this task, use a 1 or 2mm thick card (this will ensure that when the two sides are glued together, they form the correct thickness) and a sheet of clear acetate for the glass.

Transfer the window dimensions onto the sheet of card with a fine mechanical pencil; mark out two identical frames (Fig. 129). Using a sharp scalpel, cut out the panel within the frame that will hold the acetate. Use the tip of the blade to establish the corner points for precise cutting. Then with care, cut around the inner edge of each pane section, making sure not to cut through the mullions. Once cut, the pane sections should come out easily. If not, carefully run the blade in the cut groove again to ease them out.

Continue to cut around the outer edges of each frame. Place them together to check that both shapes match; and then set both aside (Fig. 130). Mark up (with allowances) and cut a piece of acetate that covers all glass panes. This is far easier than cutting out each frame individually. Apply glue sparingly in the perimeter allowance and then position it within the frame on the inside.

Using a strip of card or a small spatula, apply a small amount of glue to the inside of the window frame and firmly attach both pieces together (Fig. 131).

You can use this same technique to construct multi-panelled windows, French doors and so on. Aim to cut out the sections for glass first, before cutting around the outer edge. This will provide stability and much more precision (Fig. 132).

Note: If colour and texture is to be added, do this before gluing the acetate in place. It is far less stressful to work this way round even if you have a very steady hand.

When recreating stained glass or more complicated designs, place a piece of acetate over the technical drawing, securing it with masking tape on either side. Using a fine nibbed permanent ink pen, trace the lead or mullion pattern. If a more detailed raised surface is required, choose contour lining paste (available in any good art shop) in different colours. Illustrating markers or glass paints can be used to fill in colour.

Window furniture, such as latches, window lifts and handles can be made with wire or modelling putty in the same way as door furniture. The window should fit snugly into the wall. Apply a little glue (preferably PVA or any good wood glue if the wall is made from foam board) around the window edge and gently slide it into its correct position.

FLOORS AND CEILINGS

Depending on the purpose of the model and the level of detail needed, you can create a floor and/or ceiling detail in a number of ways. For white cut-out versions, you can draw the ceiling and floor detail on the surface or you can glue drafting prints on top. However, with fully rendered versions, a lot more information can be communicated. Design, texture and character can be added to give the model more context. Different forms of 2-D and 3-D textures can be applied to bring the model to life. These will be discussed in more detail later on in the section called: Creating Surface Treatments and Finishes.

Some models do not include ceilings, but if it is necessary, observe ceiling details like plaster work, light fixtures, ceiling roses etc. Depending on the design complexity, details can be made with materials like modelling putty, fine card or mount board.

WALLS

Walls, both interior and exterior, can have many surface treatments to represent certain architecture forms, designs, textures and materials. Other factors that create a wall's character are features such as doorframes, skirting boards, dado rails and cornicing, for example, all of which characterize period interiors. When imagining modern interiors, the possibilities are endless, and can require more ingenuity to create project-specific details.

The basic shapes for all the above can be made out of thin card or mounting board. Layering card on top of card can form the profile shapes. Alternatively, straight rods of fine wire can be used to resemble curved beading. Once glued in place, it can be painted the same colour. For curved shapes, either use wire, thin cord or contour lining paste to create fluid shapes.

CREATING SURFACE TREATMENT AND FINISHES

Interpreting surface texture to scale is an essential skill for any model maker. Experiment with various materials to find the best ways of getting the right results. The following section offers basic techniques to achieve surface features.

WOOD

There are various types of wood, each with their own characteristics – mahogany, walnut, oak, cherry, maple, pine, birch, beech and so on, and equally as many finishes for them. You can use actual wood sheeting in models, but it is unlikely to feature a scale-correct grain. So brush techniques are used to recreate the appearance of wood. Firstly, determine the wood type: what

are its characteristics? It is important to research and study the detail carefully and to have a good photograph, as reference, while you work.

The painters in the construction department will be doing the same thing. Observe the colour and the formation of the grain. Is the colour uniform? Is the grain regular? Which direction does it run in? Begin with a neutral-coloured base board. Avoid white and much darker colours such as black for the most natural effect. Apply an uneven light paint wash as a base (Fig. 133) and gradually work in darker shades to create depth. Use a range of brush sizes to create the grain detail, always working in the direction of the contours, highlighting darker grains with a darker shade of paint. Try not to let the paint dry while you work, to maintain the fluidity of the strokes.

Thin sheets of a range of wood types are also available from any good model-making shop. This form of wood is best suited for wall panels, floorboards, window shutters, doors and so on. Apply wood stain for good coverage of colour on which to build. In some cases it is best to stain large pieces to maintain a consistent tone. Once the pieces are cut, they can be retouched with paint when arranged in their final formation.

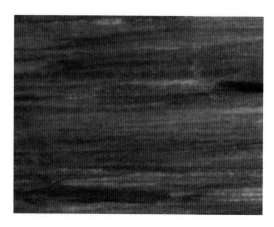

Fig. 133   Wood effect, using gouache on cartridge paper.

Creating floorboards, parquet flooring or panelling can be very time consuming, especially if the design is complex, so laboriously cutting and constructing a design piece-by-piece is not practical. Instead, try printed sheets of correctly scaled wood effects and flooring formations (from model shops). The disadvantage is that you end up with a generic rather than a specific feel.

With the growing popularity of graphic design programs, you can create unique and complex wood patterns that can be manipulated and printed out onto a variety of textured papers that meet the design requirements, much more quickly. Applying a finish to a wood or wood effect surface can add authenticity. To create a lightly polished wood look, apply an even, light layer of PVA (Fig. 134) or wood glue onto the surface. For a much heavier defined sheen, apply a varnish solution. Take note that using varnish will make colours much deeper and richer, which can be ideal to capture a period in time.

Note: depending on the size of the model and the complexity of the design, decide whether it is a good use of time to painstakingly create details. Remember, the model is not a work of art (although, they certainly can be), but a communication tool. If there is a simple way to doing something, do it, unless you are specifically requested not to.

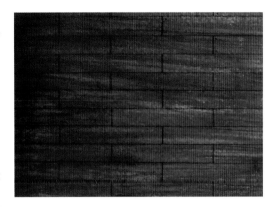

Fig. 134   Polished wood effect using PVA glue.

Fig. 135   Brickwork effect on foam board with paint. Pastels are used to work in more texture and character.

BRICKWORK

Bricks can be interpreted in both 2-D and 3-D. The 3-D methods are much more time consuming, but can capture much more feel and context than using a sheet of generic coloured bricks. This method is created using foam board. Without bending it, carefully remove the top layer of paper to expose the foam layer underneath. Using a metal ruler and a scalpel or a mechanical pencil, mark out the brickwork formation, brick by brick. This will take a while to complete, but once the formation has been defined, apply colour. Do this

with a sponge roller or spray can, taking care not to mask the brick impression (Fig. 135).

Once dry, paint to further enhance and highlight shape, form and character. There are other theatrical techniques of creating brickwork that are far more time consuming, so unless the model is actually being captured on camera, I recommend the above method for beginners. If time is short, there are many 2-D alternatives on the market, but to get a unique look, scan in photographic references or your own photographic research into a graphics program.

WALLPAPER

As wallpaper is already 2-D, there are many possibilities of achieving patterns. When selecting a print, make sure you consider scale. If both the Production Designer and Set Decorator have a design in mind, this can make the model maker's job easier. If a sizable sample is available, you can either reduce it on a photocopier (which can be time consuming), or scan it into the computer, reduce it and repeat the pattern until it fills an A4 sheet or bigger and then print it out. Make sure you print out enough copies to cover pattern returns (not all designs have straightforward pattern repeats) and wall space.

If a wallpaper pattern has yet to be decided upon, the design team should have a fairly good idea of what the designer has in mind. If no decisions have been made, the model maker may do their own research (checking that the choices are in line with the design concept and language). There is also a vast range of printed wrapping paper, which is an excellent source of patterns in convenient A2-sized sheets, which is easy to reduce in size. Use this in early conceptual stages. During pre-production it's more effective to work with the set decorating team to guide you on possible pattern samples to use (Fig. 136).

Note: overall there is always a way of achieving a surface texture through graphics packages, however, try to mix it with hand made details to avoid the coldness that 2-D can have.

TILES

Tile work used to be painstakingly recreated in much the same way as brickwork on foam board. But thankfully, the computer has turned this laborious task into a much faster and more fun task (Fig. 137).

Using a program, you can add colours and effects to a single tile shape (such as drop shadow or emboss) before it is replicated into a tile pattern. Once ready, you can print on different paper finishes to represent tile types from high glossed enamel (gloss paper) to smooth natural tiles such as stone or terracotta (semi gloss to textured). This method can also be used for linoleum.

Fig. 137   Tile floor detail.

Fig. 136   Application of wallpaper.

MARBLE

Good visual research observing colour formation, features and finish is vital for marble effects (Fig. 138). This will guide you towards the right texture base before applying colour. Experiment with different paint washes and brush techniques to create a marble effect.

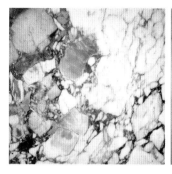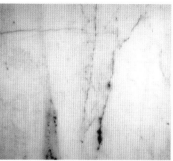

Fig. 138   Types of marble.

As always there are numerous 2-D variations available in shops and from graphic software. Consider the surface effect of the marble before heading down this road. Not all marble is smooth and polished, so why not experiment with a traditional medium such as paint washes to recreate this effect?

GLASS

Representing glass to scale is easy, with sheets of acetate. A single piece can be sandwiched between two frames to create a glass effect. For a frosted effect, use frosted acetate, a sheet of tracing paper or place a strip of double-sided adhesive tape between two layers of clear acetate. Work a round-ended tool into the plastic, distorting it to achieve the effect of textured glass.

Stained glass is hard to realize small scale. Intricate designs can be translated onto the acetate with fine-nibbed permanent pens. Alternatively, you can photocopy or print intricate designs directly on to acetate. Not all acetate is printable, so check before you buy it. For working in scale, I would suggest printing designs on the computer. This way, the design retains its scale, whereas a photocopier will distort it. When adding colour either use illustrating markers or glass paints. Depending on the intricacy, you may need to use a fine brush when applying the paint.

METAL

Nowadays, there are many types of metal that are pliable enough for model work. Many metallic-effect surfaces, such as industrial or mechanical forms can be achieved. Metals such as copper, brass, aluminium, nickel silver, steel and tin come in pliable solid sheets, mesh, tubing and rod (useful for piping) forms for convenience. All forms can be cut with a pair of metal cutters or a fine jigsaw. All of these are available from any good model shop, however, if you use vast quantities it can become prohibitively expensive.

Metal foils, such as kitchen foil can be a cheaper alternative. You can glue it to a surface and apply metal paint to give it character. Sheet foil also picks up texture – it can be smoothed over an uneven surface to create an interesting quality that can then be enhanced with paint. Mesh work or wire work can be created with varying thicknesses of wire soldered together to represent grill or fence work.

STONE

The surface quality of stone can vary from smooth to rough, sharp-edged to curved, or craggy. Depending on the form and effect desired, consider whether it is better to create the effect in 2-D or 3-D. Stone tiles and smooth surfaces can be easily achieved effectively on screen. For more textured forms, use multi-purpose polyfiller (available from DIY stores). Spread it onto thick card or wood, and work it in to add textural character before it dries. Once dry, use sandpaper to smooth out and shape uneven surfaces. Use a dry paintbrush with undiluted gouache to add colour and decay – apply it to crevices to enhance the form.

CONTEXT EFFECTS

Creating perfectly made models is crucial for a model-maker, however, applying character and context is just as essential. The Production Designer's concept needs to be realized at every stage of the design process. Setting the scene is of the utmost importance whether it is during pre-production or when you pitch for the job. As has been mentioned throughout this book, many elements come together to create design, and these must be carried on through this process.

Much time and effort is expended in researching each set and as a model maker, you need to pay attention to this research. Who inhabits this space? How old is it? How long have they been there? What is the purpose of the space? Is it still functioning in the same way as was originally intended? What is the narrative situation?

By observing the documented research, you will see how surfaces and spaces are intended to look. When a character is added to a space, it tells us more about it. By experimenting with various aging, wear and tear, deterioration from other elements (consider how surfaces react when exposed to extremes of temperature, water, fire and so on) techniques put the space in context.

Fig. 139 Applying wear and tear to create context detail.

Use photographs as reference to see how different factors affect surfaces. For example, when wallpaper is exposed to constant sunlight, it fades. When exposed to moisture it peels, stains and grows mouldy; paint flakes and metal rusts.

Apply watered-down brown paint, or strong coffee or tea to create the effect of water stains on wallpaper. Once the paper absorbs the water, it alters its shape, giving the model context. All spaces have varying amount of history, down to the layers of plaster, paint or wallpaper applied to its surfaces. Consider this when creating wall coverings. Experiment with varying textural layers to add authenticity.

Apply a little paint straight from the tube onto a dry brush with strong bristles to help add more texture. Highlight forms by adding darker colours into corners and crevices (Fig. 139). Soft chalk pastels are also ideal. Add a bit of colour and work into the surface with your index finger, making sure to blend it in. Each treated surface responds to age and decay is different ways, so photographic reference material will help guide you.

FURNITURE

When making furniture, again, time is the deciding factor. Consider how much detail you need. Do you have to include all the furniture, or just the main pieces? Whatever the answer, try to learn basic forms, which can be worked on for more detail.

CHAIRS AND SOFAS

Depending on the style and shape of the chair, select the material closest to its appearance. If the chair is a simple metal frame with wooden seat and back, choose a pliable wire for the frame and either balsa wood or mount board for the seat and back. Wooden chairs can be made with either balsa wood or mount board. The method below can be adapted for most forms of chair.

Task 3: Make a Model Chair

Begin with drafting out the components on paper on a scale of 1:25 or ¼": 1' as shown in Fig. 140. Then transfer the measurements onto mount board or balsa wood.

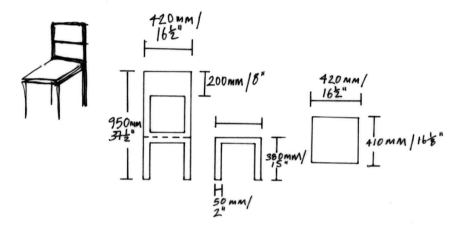

Fig. 140   Basic chair dimensions.

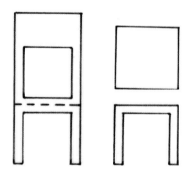

With a sharp scalpel cut out pieces A, B, and C. Using a multi-purpose glue, apply just enough to the top of piece C and attach it firmly to a width edge of piece B. Allow to set at a right angle. Once dry, apply glue to the opposite end of piece B and attach it to piece A. Stand the chair on its legs to make sure it is level, then rest on its side to dry completely (Fig. 141). When dry, apply paint.

Fig. 141   Chair in pieces.

Living room seating tends to have more curves and softer edges. So balsa wood or mount board alone will not achieve the desired look. You can create the base with mount board, but then you need a more pliable material on top to create a soft look. Foam board with the top layer of paper removed can be used to form shape, by carving into it with a scalpel, or alternatively use epoxy modelling putty to build up the form. Using model-making tools, define the shape, cushions, and studs that are characteristic of soft furniture. Once complete, either allow to air dry or leave it to harden in a hot oven. Once hardened, it can be glued to the mount board base and then painted with acrylic paint.

Task 4: Create a Model Table

Construct a table following the same principles as described above. For the best results use either wood or mount board for solid worktops and acetate for glass.

Draft out the table top and legs as shown in Fig. 142 in either scale 1:25 or ¼": 1'. Transfer the measurements onto chosen the chosen material and cut all pieces out.

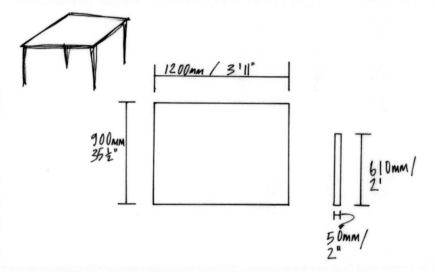

Fig. 142   Basic table dimensions.

Fig. 143   Chair and table constructed.

Place the tabletop upside down and using enough glue, attach all four legs at right angles to the tabletop corners (Fig. 143). Once dried, apply paint.

DESKS AND SIDEBOARDS

Desks, sideboards, cupboards and cabinets consist of varying combinations of block forms. Observe their shapes to work out the best way of creating them.

Task 5: Create a Simple Desk

In this case, the desk is made of two block-like pedestals with a desktop fitted on top. Construct two blocks with the specified dimensions in either 1:25 or ¼ ": 1' scale in Fig. 144.

Cut out and glue each block together, noticing that each block should have no top or bottom. Cut out the desktop and place it wrong side up. Apply glue to the tops of the block tops, and place them on the desktop, so that they sit flush with the edges (Fig. 145). Once dry, apply paint. Adapt this method to suit the specific object.

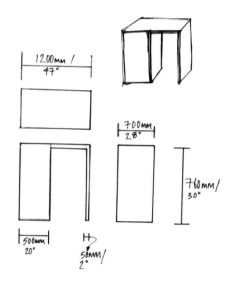

ABOVE: Fig. 144   Basic desk dimensions.

LEFT: Fig. 145   Desk constructed.

Task 5: Create a Bookcase

Start with a box shape to form shelves and bookcase. Draft out the five sections in card, and measure and cut out all shelves (choose a thinner card for these).

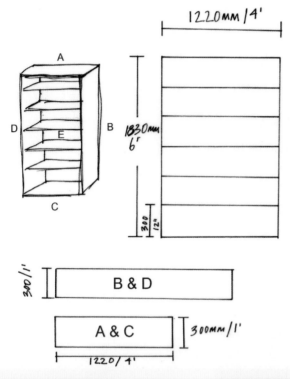

Refer to Fig. 146. Remember to check that each shelf is the same width as E and the same depth as B and D. Before constructing, draw faint shelf guidelines on E. Now attach all pieces and set aside to dry. Apply just enough glue to each shelf depth and width edges (three sides only). Using a pair of tweezers (Fig. 147), insert each shelf in line with the faint guidelines. Leave to dry, and apply colour.

Fig. 146   Bookshelf dimensions.

Fig. 147   Glue shelves using model-making tweezers.

Fig. 148 and Fig. 149 Designer Cecily Duckett has used a variety of textured materials along with tissue paper and modelling putty to achieve a high level of detail.

BATHROOM FURNITURE

Baths, sinks and toilets are best created with modelling putty. Trying to create a curved 3-D form on a small scale is very difficult and time consuming. Modelling putty is an easier way to create any style, which can then be painted and glazed or sprayed with glass paint for that recognizable sheen.

FINER DETAILS

As you have seen, working in scale requires a little ingenuity to find different materials that represent

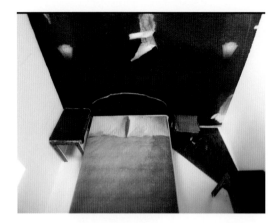

Fig. 150   This illustrates how effective the use of 2-D images applied to 3-D shapes can be.

2-D DETAIL

Expressing thoughts and ideas in two dimensions can be quick and effective. It takes time to create fine details such as rows of books on a shelf, or detailed carpet, so either use scaled-down photos or computer graphics for the best effect. When applying 2-D detail, consider the effect just using computer imagery can have on a 3-D space.

Try combining handmade elements with computer images for a more well balanced, authentic look. Always consider the most visually effective look, rather than choosing the easy way out. Fig. 150 shows how applying photographic images onto 3-D objects and in space can be very effective in achieving a look and feel, in this case decay.

SCALE PERSON

Any model needs a scaled figure to add context and comparison. In theatre models, these are

objects in a scale form. For example, glass beads can be threaded onto wire to for chandeliers. Fabrics can give furniture a more textural effect. Figs 148 and 149 show how different materials can make models more realistic. Observe the foam on the sofas and the felt on the carpet. Notice how it adds contrast to the stone fireplace and the parquet flooring.

Fig. 151   A 2-D human form creates an effective presence in a model. (Designer: Natasha Moses)

Fig. 152   A series of photographs of the model using simple light sources to create ambience.

made with a wire frame, and then covered with modelling putty to take on human form. Screen models do this, however, a 2-D representation is far more likely. On some technical drawings, a draughtsperson will indicate a human form, so it is best to use their dimensions as a guide. Draft out the dimensions of the figure onto mount board and the semi-circle stand. Add as much detail as you like to the form. Cut a 2mm-slit in the middle of the figure, and do the same with the stand. Avoid cutting right through it. Fit the cut grooved pieces together so that the figure can stand. If a 3-D form is more desirable, use the same figure dimensions as guidance, but create the form with pliable wire. Apply modelling putty to create

the form. In Fig. 151, the designer has used a human form from a magazine to add a touch of realism.

PHOTOGRAPHING A MODEL

Capturing a model in different lighting states is a very theatrical practice. However, it is a good exercise to see how a set can be used and captured on camera. Simple apparatus such as an Anglepoise lamp®, and torchlight can create atmosphere. Fig. 152 shows how varying lighting states and framing of the camera help to create an almost life-like feel. Organized in sequence, the images can create a very effective storyboard.

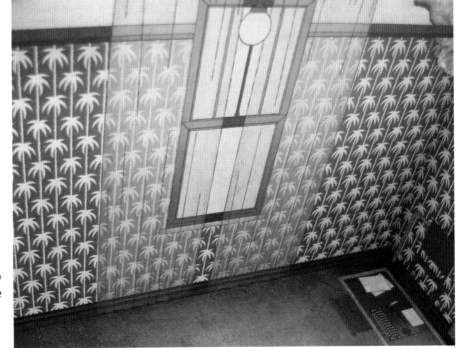

Figs 153 to 156 Designer Alessandro Vitali creates 2-D perspective images in the 3-D space.

When putting ideas forward for a pitch, a good model that captures the atmosphere of a project can have a great visual impact that can lead to you winning the job.

When presenting ideas for a pitch, think how the work will be communicated. What will have the most impact and be the most memorable? Take your time to organize research, ideas and design, which will assist the explanation. Figs 157 to 159 show how a model and mood boards can be presented. Each component complements the other to show a clear strong concept and style. Observe how the colour palette flows from the research through to the model, and how the layout provides a way of communicating the ideas clearly.

When explaining design ideas, the key is to come across as confident and enthused, but never overconfident. Remember, you are not only selling your ideas, but you are also presenting yourself as the right candidate for the job. The more confident and comfortable you feel about your work, your skill and your ability to work as a team member, the more suitable you are.

For the pitch process, there is always the question of how detailed you should make your design,

Task 5: Experiment with Light

Experiment with different-coloured lighting states by holding gels in front of the light. First, have the light in front, and then position the light from behind (back light) and then from the side. Observe what the light does to the set. Stage lighting differs greatly from screen lighting, as there are more subtleties involved.

However, consider the feel that practical (on-set) light provides and how it affects the space. When making a model always consider how and at what stage it will be presented.

as there is no guarantee that you will be offered the job. So it's really up to you how comfortable you are about producing detailed ideas. The best advice is to look at each pitch or presentation as experience or practice.

Figs 157 to 159   Presenting the model and the mood board, in a clever and exciting way.

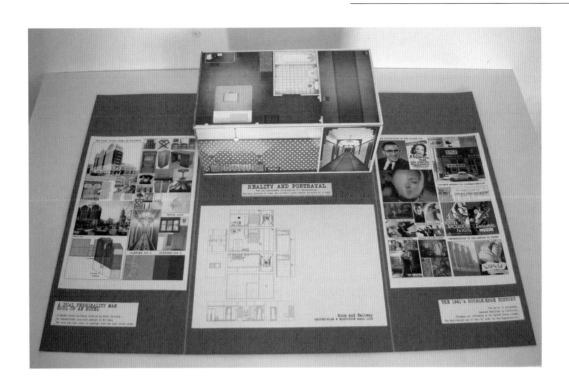

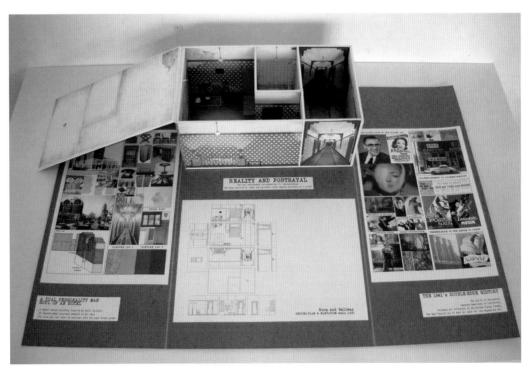

Development

• Production Designer • Supervising Art Director • Art Director • Assistant Art Director • Draughts Person • Concept Artist • Illustrator • Model Maker • Art Department Coordinator • Art Department • Assistant Set Designer • Junior Draughtsman • Construction Manager • Carpenter • Painter • Scenic Painter • Set Decorator • Production Buyer • Assistant Set Decorator • Props Master • Drapesman • Prop Maker • Set Dresser • Standby Set Dresser • Greensman • Swing Gang • Home Economist • Weapons Master • Production Designer • Supervising Art Director • Art Director • Assistant Art Director • Draughts Person • Concept Artist • Illustrator • Model Maker • Art Department Coordinator • Art Department • Assistant Set Designer • Junior Draughtsman • Construction Manager • Carpenter • Painter • Scenic Painter • Set Decorator • Production Buyer • Assistant Set Decorator • Props Master • Drapesman • Prop Maker • Set Dresser • Standby Set Dresser • Greensman • Swing Gang • Home Economist • Weapons Master • Production Designer • Supervising Art Director • Art Director • Assistant Art Director • Draughts Person • Concept Artist • Illustrator • Model Maker • Art Department Coordinator • Art Department •

Pre-Production

• Assistant Set Designer • Junior Draughtsman • Construction Manager • Carpenter • Painter • Scenic Painter • Set Decorator • Production Buyer • Assistant Set Decorator • Props Master • Drapesman • Prop Maker • Set Dresser • Standby Set Dresser • Greensman • Swing Gang • Home Economist • Weapons Master • Production Designer • Supervising Art Director • Art Director • Assistant Art Director • Draughts Person • Concept Artist • Illustrator • Model Maker • Art Department Coordinator • Art Department • Assistant Set Designer • Junior Draughtsman • Construction Manager • Carpenter • Painter • Scenic Painter • Set Decorator • Production Buyer • Assistant Set Decorator • Props Master • Drapesman • Prop Maker • Set Dresser •

In Production

• Standby Set Dresser • Greensman • Swing Gang • Home Economist • Weapons Master • Production Designer • Supervising Art Director • Art Director • Assistant Art Director • Draughts Person • Concept Artist • Illustrator • Model Maker • Art Department Coordinator • Art Department • Assistant Set Designer • Junior Draughtsman • Construction Manager • Carpenter • Painter • Scenic Painter • Set Decorator • Production Buyer • Assistant Set Decorator • Props Master • Drapesman • Prop Maker • Set Dresser • Standby Set Dresser • Greensman • Swing Gang • Home Economist • Weapons Master • Production Designer • Supervising Art Director • Art Director • Assistant Art Director • Draughts Person • Concept Artist • Illustrator • Model Maker • Art Department Coordinator • Art Department • Assistant Set Designer • Junior Draughtsman • Construction Manager • Carpenter • Painter • Scenic Painter • Set Decorator • Production Buyer • Assistant Set Decorator • Props Master • Drapesman • Prop Maker • Set Dresser • Standby Set Dresser • Greensman • Swing Gang • Home Economist • Production Designer • Supervising Art Director • Art Director • Assistant Art Director • Draughts Person • Set Designer •

Post Production

•

9 The Production Process

TEAMWORK

For anyone who has experienced some form of filming, one thing is for sure, it is all consuming, and patience is a virtue! Anyone who has started out in film or television will have experienced the production process. Whether it was working on graduate films or no or low budget films, you will have seen a production team at work. It is symbiotic relationship, a well-oiled machine that works together seamlessly. This chapter will discuss all the key activities of the production process.

It may be surprising to anyone unfamiliar with the business, how time-consuming the shooting process is. The captured images are what teams work tirelessly for; it is a slow, methodical process which will be explained in more detail under the heading Production/In Production. When crewing up, heads of departments look for people who are skilled, and have the right attitude to work as team players.

Filming is always pressured, so it's essential to have team members that can deal with that pressure. Tempers can flare but the key is to never let it affect your work. If your work is criticised, it is important not to go to pieces, but to take it on board and move on... This is all part of the experience. Remember too, that your reputation is important, as you will get more work through word of mouth.

The production process of any film, television, or video project generally follows a four-stage process: development; pre production; production and post-production. The duration of each stage will vary greatly, depending on whether it is a feature film, television feature-length drama, television series, a music video or a commercial. The scale of the production is most important – the broader the vision, the bigger the budget and the problems. Preparation and shooting time can also differ greatly depending on the type of project. Developing and shooting a commercial or music video can take up to two or three weeks. A feature film may have six to ten weeks preparation plus six to ten weeks of shooting, while a television series can have eight weeks preparation time and six to eight weeks shoot.

WHO'S WHO

The size of the production crew depends on the size of the production and can vary greatly. The bigger the vision, the more people are needed to make it happen. A production is made up of different groups of people all working to a common goal. They include the production company or studio and producers who put up the funding and monitor expenditure throughout the process.

The production has a number of specific depart-

OPPOSITE: **Fig. 160** Design by the author.

ments that perform key business functions, such as accounts, payroll, legal, financial, planning, scheduling, and eventual distribution. The Director is employed by the production company and sits above the following departments.

THE DESIGN CREW

The design crew is responsible for anything visible on screen. They are headed up by the Production Designer. This is explained in detail below.

THE SHOOTING CREW

Responsible for the captured image, the shooting crew includes the DoP, the camera crew, the electrical department and sound production, and on-set art department.

THE CAST

Without the cast, there would be no story!

THE EDITING TEAM

The editing team consists of the Editor, Colourist or Grader (responsible for adjusting all shot footage, so that it remains consistent) and Sound Designers.

ART DEPARTMENT: THE DESIGN TEAM

PRODUCTION DESIGNER

This is the name given to the person responsible for the overall look and feel of any filmed project for film, television, video, music video and commercial. They are visual storytellers, who communicate emotion and atmosphere to support the story's narrative. Through conceptualization and realization, they create sound stage sets and choose and change locations to fit the project's visual concept. They have the objective artistic and design integrity to know what suits the story best. They are versatile artists who can adapt their design skills to suit each individual project. As artists, they must also be practical and cost conscious, as they need to create wondrous environments under time and budget pressure.

The Production Designer interacts with many departments across the production. However, they work very closely with the Director, Producer, and the DoP (Director of Photography). Establishing a good working relationship early is essential for success, as Designer Luciana Arrighi explains:

> I very closely work with the Director to get on his wave length, and be able to read his mind; so that by the time we film; there is hardly need to query further. Working through the script and later joined by the DoP. We are then the creative three.
>
> (Interview with author, 2011)

Through regular discussions with these key players, the designer can gain valuable information on how the script is being interpreted, as well as identifying themes, locations and environments that will be integral to the overall design. They decide on the project's visual language – its style and look and feel that supports the storytelling. Presenting a unified front is crucial and emphasizes that the entire team is working towards the common goal.

Depending on the size of the project, the Production Designer works at quite a high level. On smaller projects with lower budgets, the Production Designer and the Art Director may be the same person, whereas on larger projects this is impossible. They rely heavily on the Supervising Art Director and the art department to make things happen. This is why Production Designers like to choose an art director that will meet their expectations on every level. They monitor the work that the Art Director carries out in translating conceptual ideas into fully functional sets and manage the process and schedule.

In addition to the Art Director and art department, the Production Designer works with the wardrobe department; with hair and make-up; visual effects (VFX) and special effects (SFX) teams (to make sure that specific set-ups and blue screens are correctly positioned to help in post-production); sound crew (to ensure understanding of the set's acoustics, and agree on set microphone placement); second units, production office, Assistant Directors; transport and post-production.

They report to the Line Producer (LP) on budget expenditure and communicate with the LP and Assistant Directors on the schedule. Therefore, it is vital for the Production Designer to delegate. Many Production Designers work differently, some draft or draw but there is a point when they have to step away and take on more of an overall management role to be effective. It would be physically impossible for them to do everything. Designer Ken Adam is a strong believer in surrounding oneself with talented crew members, as he describes:

> …That cliché, 'You're only as good as your team' – it's partly true. You still have to come up with the ideas and guide the team to realize it… Whereas with good assistants you can allocate a lot of responsibility.
> (Ken Adam – *The Art of Production Design*, p. 294).

SUPERVISING* ART DIRECTOR OR ART DIRECTOR

The Art Director's job remains the same no matter what the project: to support and execute the visual language as stipulated by the Production Designer and Director. The Art Director reports directly to the Production Designer and is either completely or partially responsible for the all work produced in a number of departments (art department, construction department, set decorating, location and visual effects). They are responsible for all construction work on set in studio and on location along with the Set Decorator.

Art Directors are highly skilled practitioners. They have a variety of skills that cover most, if not all, aspects of an art department's function. They need good communication skills and a competent knowledge of screen design; an in-depth knowledge of modern and period architecture; script analysis; construction; drafting; cameras (both film and digital); film stocks; lighting and a knowledge of the strengths and weaknesses of computer applications.

They may be required to interpret a Production Designer's conceptual drawings in draft form before handing them over as guidance to the Assistant Art Director and draughtspeople. In addition to these creative skills, they must also have good managerial skills. These are all essential attributes when it comes to scheduling because so much has to be looked out for during pre-production and production. They share budget and scheduling responsibilities with the Producer and First Assistant Director. Art Directors are heavily involved in the selection and employment of all art department personnel along with the Art Department Coordinator.

ON-SET ART DIRECTOR

The on-set Art Director is responsible for the on-set art department. He or she will remain on set for the entire shoot, to manage the standby props person, standby painter, standby carpenter, and rigger. If any issues arise during shooting, it is the role of the on-set Art Director to find solutions and to feed

---

*The term Supervising Art Director is used to distinguish the head of the department, when there are several Art Directors. On big productions they may be two or three Art Directors, who divide up and manage the various locations, set builds and foreign locations.

back any issues to the Supervising Art Director and Production Designer.

ASSISTANT ART DIRECTORS

Again, depending on the size of the production there may be one, two or three Assistant Art Directors. The aim is for an Assistant Art Director to progress to Art Director, so they should aspire to have the same experience and knowledge as an Art Director. Essentially, they carry out the Art Director's instructions.

Their responsibilities include set drafting, location surveying, sourcing materials, researching and collecting information for the Art Director and Production Designer, and outfitting sets with hardware (that is, knowledge of period and modern styles and features such as doors and windows and so on, how they work and are constructed). They must also have practical art department experience and knowledge, and be able to understand production schedules. They should communicate well with the construction crews, and be problem solvers.

DRAUGHTSMAN AND SET DESIGNERS

There will be a number of Set Designers, depending on the production. They are responsible for drafting up all sets and structures for studio spaces and locations.

JUNIOR DRAUGHTSMAN

A junior draughtsman has key skills, and is given details to draft, such as windows and doors, for example. This is a way to gain valuable practical experience. They tend to move up the ranks when they show initiative and efficiency in their craft.

CONCEPT ARTISTS AND ILLUSTRATORS

These artists work closely with the Production Designer and Director, visually interpreting and communicating their ideas. They tend to start work before the Art Director.

GRAPHICS

Graphic Designers produce all graphic material caught on camera.

MODEL MAKER

The Model Maker is responsible for interpreting drafting plans and 2-D conceptual visuals creating scaled models, with varying degrees of detail, from simplistic white card cut-outs to highly rendered models.

ART DEPARTMENT COORDINATOR

The Art Department Co-ordinator ensures the smooth running of the department. They coordinate with the Art Director or Supervising Art Director on recruitment, assist in clearing copyright for brand logos, company names and anything else that needs permission to be shown on screen.

ART DEPARTMENT ASSISTANT

Art Department Assistants tend to be studio-based, looking after the print and issuing all drawings to the construction department. They also produce art department graphics, order art department supplies and look after petty cash purchases. They support the Art Department Coordinator and the team, and can be called upon to assist in any aspect of the art department's function. Many people who want to work in the art department, but are unsure in what capacity, begin as assistants, and then specialize.

SET DECORATOR

The Set Decorator works very closely with the Production Designer, interpreting their ideas through all forms of decoration and prop selection. The Set Decorator needs to be creatively in tune with the Production Designer so that they can interpret the Production Designer's creative vision. They must also be able to analyse a script and break it down, read technical drafting, and must have a good knowledge of modern and period architecture, styles, furniture, fabrics, prints, fixtures and fittings. They must be able to visualize characters, as they are often decorating and dressing their environments.

Along with the Supervising Art Director, the Set Decorator is jointly responsible for all construction and decoration work on set and on location. The Set Decorator heads up the team that dresses the set – everything that is visible on screen is the responsibility of the Set Decorator. As a head of department, he or she is responsible for budget estimation and monitoring. In the early stages of pre-production, the Set Decorator and the team are out on the road collating visual reference material for discussions with the Production Designer. The Decorator will bring sample variations of an element, such as wallpaper, for example, to the table for the Designer and Decorator to discuss which variation is best.

PRODUCTION BUYER

Working closely with the Set Decorator, the Production Buyer is responsible for the sourcing, purchasing and hiring of all set dressing, hero or action props for each set. The Buyer is also responsible for controlling the budget. On smaller productions the buyer may double up as the Assistant Set Decorator.

SET DECORATING ASSISTANT

This person supports both the Set Decorator and the Production Buyer. Like the Decorator and Buyer, they are out on the road sourcing and purchasing dressing and arranging pick-ups for props. They are given a cash float, which they must be able to account for.

SET DRESSERS

Set Dressers report to the Set Decorator and are under their guidance. The Set Dressers, also known as the Swing Gang, are responsible for the applica-

tion of all set decoration (in line with the creative vision of the Set Decorator), including everything from furniture, soft furnishings to picture hanging and flower arranging. (Should the set require more plant life, a Greensman and crew will be employed to manage, dress and creatively arrange live and artificial plants.)

Once shooting on a particular set has been completed or wrapped, the team return to remove or strike the set. Much care and attention should be taken when removing dressing from a set, as not all pieces will have been purchased. Some will have been hired, so the dressers must be careful not to damage any articles, as any damage will come out of the Set Decorator's budget.

During the shoot, there will be one On-set or Standby Set Dresser who will can reset any dressing for another take or shot. They should be observant and have a good eye for detail, as correct prop resetting provides the continuity in each shot, making the editor's job a lot easier during post-production.

HOME ECONOMIST

The Home Economist is responsible for all the food and drink on screen. They produce and supply edible action food and dressing food, along with non-alcoholic beverages as a substitute for alcohol on set. Preparing dressing food requires skill and experience, to create authentic dishes that can survive the heat of the lights on set. The home economist must have a good knowledge of period and modern food and beverages and how they were prepared and served, as well as preservation techniques.

PROPS

Working closely with the set decorating department, the Prop Master is head of the property department, and is responsible for delivery, storage and return of all props, whether it is purchased for the production or hired out. He or she will organize all prop deliveries and pick ups to and from all set locations.

The props store is divided into individual set areas that will include everything that has been purchased or hired for it. It is the responsibility of the Props Storeman to maintain the order of each set dressing area and to update an inventory list, which the Props Master will oversee. The props department has its own props truck driver who will transport all dressing to and from a set's location.

On set there will be a Chargehand Standby Propman and a Standby Propman. The Chargehand Propman will be in charge of all props on set, especially hero props and the Standby Propman will assist with anything relating to props during the shooting process.

DRAPESMAN

The Drapesman is responsible for curtains, cushions, upholstery, and all soft furnishings. They are skilled sewers and have a good eye for quality and detail.

PROPS MAKER

This person creates the props that have been specifically designed for a production. They will be skilled in many forms of construction (electronics and technical engineering) and will be familiar with various materials, such as plastic and fibreglass.

WEAPONS MASTER

As the term implies, he or she is responsible for all functioning weapons on set and will have certified training and licences.

CONSTRUCTION MANAGER

The Construction Manager works closely with the (Supervising) Art Director and the Set Decorator, and oversees all the set construction. The manager is responsible for ordering all building materials and is also reliant on the set decorating depart-

ment for materials, such as wallpaper, specific paints, tiles and so on. The Manager will organize and oversee the often sizable construction crews, ensuring that the work is progressing to schedule.

Depending on the requirements, the construction crew will be made up of different departments, each with a head of department, such as carpentry and joinery, painters (including specialized paint applications to create and age surfaces, such as wood, marble, metal and stone) plasterers, wood machinists, stagehands (do a variety of supporting jobs for the construction crews) and scenic artists (who produce painted scenic backgrounds and cycloramas).

SPECIAL EFFECTS DEPARTMENT

This team introduces alternative effects to recreate situations or scenarios that are too costly or risky to try during a live shoot. Practical (mechanical, such as earthquake simulation, hydraulics) and physical (such as snow, rain, explosions, fire and so on) effects are designed and created to perform the scenario in a controlled environment.

CAMERA, LIGHTING AND FILM STOCK KNOWLEDGE

It is important to know the screen ratio, as this will affect how you design your set. It is always good to work through the language of the project with the Director and the DoP, the type of lenses. It may mean sitting down with the Director and DoP having initial discussions over other films focusing on whether static or fluid shots are appropriate and how they will be lit. Discussing lenses, stock tests, certain lighting, and how colours and textures react to stock and lighting (how they react under tungsten or day lighting).

Aging effects can be worked out through storyboards. One can make decisions on whether the camera is in the right position and proximity to pick up the detail. It is important that everyone presents a united front and supports the vision of the production. Pooling information and expertise about cameras, lenses and stock helps to get the job done. As a Designer you learn the importance of considering every means of lighting. Artificially lighting a set can make it appear realistic on screen. This is why you test stock and discuss their effects and agree on the 'look'.

Production Designers look at photography and painting, among other things, for inspiration. Photography is of great value, as it possesses the captured image, the lighting and the film used to achieve the subject matter. The quality of the image captured may differ, but a near perfect feel can be replicated through film and digital cameras.

DEVELOPMENT

When a production is said to be In Development, it means that it is in its very early stages and nothing is confirmed. The script might still be in need of work, especially if a Producer and Director have been working on the project at this stage. Funding is also a consideration at this point. Some projects remain in development limbo for months, even years, because funding cannot be secured (possibly because of the nature of the script or its marketability). Having a known Director or actor linked with the project will interest investors, who want to avoid taking risks. However, this should not scare off smaller independent projects with lower budgets. They may struggle to get funding, but can, and often do, produce amazingly innovative work. There is pressure for a big production to keep to the agreed budget and turn a healthy profit and companies often choose the safer option or a remake, which can be disappointing.

Funding is paramount. Without it the project will struggle. Sometimes assigning a particular Director, actor or Production Designer early on can have a huge impact on funding. With bankable crew and cast members, production companies are more willing to agree funding, because they know that it is a likely to be a solid investment and the likelihood of a healthy profit is high. A project can take years to get off the ground for any of the various reasons mentioned.

PRE-PRODUCTION

When a project moves into the pre-production phase, it is preparing for the shooting stage. This is the most important period for the Production Designer and the design and construction team. A lot has to be accomplished in this phase; everything from 2-D conceptual design to constructed sets completed with dressing, all within budget and on schedule. It is a tall order. Crucially, planning must take place before anything can begin.

The cast will need to be finalized. There will be screen tests, with the Director. The DoP will work closely with the Production Designer and the art department. Once the cast is confirmed, colours may be changed to work with them, their skin tones and so on. A change of cast can also impact how the DoP lights them.

A Production Designer is brought on just before pre-production and will be involved in discussions with the Director, the Producer and DoP. They will be making decisions about the project's visual language and style. They already have a conceptual artist on board who will be able to help the group with imagery. The Production Designer carries on researching and drawing, to get a handle on the overall look and feel, before coming back to the table for further discussions.

Once everyone is in agreement, schedule and budgets are agreed before work can begin. The (Supervising) Art Director, Construction Manager, Set Decorator, and Costume Designer should be on board at this stage. They all have to be involved in the budgeting and schedule process for it to be realistic.

BUDGETS AND SCHEDULING: MAINTAINING A HOLD ON PRIORITIES

Before pre-production (pre-pre-production) can get into full swing, many elements need to come together in creating fully functioning sets. The Production Designer's job is to put together a practical and realistic schedule that all design departments will follow. The production schedule is based upon the shooting schedule, drawn up by the Unit Production Manager with input from the Production Designer, DoP and First Assistant Director. A project is rarely shot in sequence, as it is not an economical use of time, so each set or location will be organized in a practical order to cover all scenes that take place on each set. They will be divided into day and night scenes, as the lighting set-ups will need to change and that takes time. The shooting dates predetermine each set's completion deadline for all the design and construction departments.

From these dates the Production Designer and the (Supervising) Art Director work backwards to work out when to begin each stage. Both must be able to estimate how much time it will take to create each set – which means having a good understanding of time taken to design, draft, build, paint, decorate and dress each set. Both the Production Designer and Art Director should communicate regularly with the Unit Production Manager to check on progress. Once the schedule has been agreed, the Supervising Art Director assumes responsibility for meeting the set production deadlines, he or she must communicate information to all departments. The Production Designer assumes a more overall supervisory role.

Drawing up the budget is an essential part of the planning and scheduling process. The Production Designer along with the (Supervising) Art Director, Construction Manager, Set Decorator and Costume Designer sit down with each department's estimated budget and meticulously work out the cost for each set. The budget should be approached based on the requirements of the script and how many studio and location builds are required. This information determines each set and the estimated cost. If the figure is above what the producer expected, savings will have to be made. This can be a contentious issue. There has been a feeling across the film and television industries, that Producers have little idea of the true cost of running an art department and the numbers of people needed to create elaborate sets. Production Designer, Jane Morton recalls:

> I remember a producer coming up to me saying…but it's only for TV!
>
> (Interview with author, 2011)

As a Designer, it doesn't matter whether it is television, film or commercial; basic costs need to be budgeted for. The Production Designer sits with the Art Director, Construction Manager, Set Decorator and Costume Designer to agree each department's needs and estimates the costs. Each department produces a budget breakdown of the art department, construction, decoration, props, wardrobe and make-up, and locations and studio hires.

Each department budget should include the number of crew members and their salaries, including expenses, costs for materials, equipment, purchase and hire, loss and damage, and miscellaneous, which is the contingency that must be built in to cover any unexpected costs. Any loss or damage has to come out of the budget, so it is advisable to estimate higher, rather than lower. Once the budgets are confirmed, each department head is responsible for managing their own budget under the careful eye of the Production Designer. At this stage the art department, construction and decorating crews begin to take shape. On a film, the costume department starts a little later than the art department, whereas for television and smaller projects the costume department starts at the same time because the pre-production process is much shorter. Once all departments are up and running, the (Supervising) Art Director takes over and manages the workload and productivity of the departments, so that it is to schedule and within budget. The script is not completely finished during pre-production; it will still be worked on and amendments may be made.

New script pages will be circulated to all the departments, colour coded, so that all the crew know which is the most up-to-date version and which pages have been substituted. The script drives the project and can have a huge impact on the work of the art department, construction and decoration.

All departments should work in harmony and communicate well and make sure that the decisions made are filtered down to the relevant people. This is the most exciting time for the Screen Designer and teams, as the 2-D conceptual ideas take form and come to life.

PRODUCTION/IN PRODUCTION

When the pre-production phase has ended, the project moves into the shooting phase, where the Director, Production Designer, DoP and camera crew, cast, Gaffer and lighting crew, sound, special effects, and on-set art department begin to capture each shot in line to schedule.

When schedules are tight, as they often are, shooting and set construction will run concurrently. Once a set has been finished, the shooting team moves in and the art department and construction crews move onto the next one, and so on. This is why the on-set art department for a film or television project needs to be made up of separate crew members as there is far too much ground to cover for the art department crew.

After each day of shooting, dailies or rushes are usually made available for the Director, DoP, Production Designer, Set Decorator and Costume Designer and Producer, to view and review. The rushes normally come with some kind of soundtrack that allows the Director and crew to study every element of shooting, from actor position, lighting, set, textures, continuity, booms to checking that other elements are out of shot, and so on. Decisions about the developing or colour balance/quality of the light will be made. If changes need to be made they are done so swiftly, as they will need to be re-shot, and will have an impact on the shooting schedule.

When the shooting phase is in full swing, the majority of the art department crew finish on the job. They heads of department stay on till the shoot wraps, when all sets are dismantled, hire props are returned, and purchased ones are stored (in case re-shoots are needed) and all the paperwork is signed off.

POST-PRODUCTION

This is the phase that the project moves into, when shooting has been completed or wrapped. The Director sits down with the Editor and begins to piece the story together. Visual effects, Colourists, and Sound Designers are heavily employed at this phase to ensure that all elements fit together seamlessly. The Producer and production company become more involved in the final stages, as it nears the marketing stage, where the production company will ensure it reaches its final destination – theatrical release, cinema screen, or television screen. Music videos and commercials have a faster turnaround time compared to film and television dramas. Films and television dramas are released the following year.

Glossary

Blocking – the planning of the actors' and camera's positions and movements in preparation for shooting.

CGI – Computer Generated Imagery.

Cut – what the Director says to stop the camera rolling. Also, an editing term, meaning the immediate change from one shot to another; a piece of film either of a single scene or a series of scenes. It can also refer to a version of the entire film, as in rough cut, final cut or Director's cut.

Dailies – also known as rushes, refers to the raw footage of a day's filming processed in the lab and delivered either at the end of or the next day, hence the name. The footage has been developed simply for speed, synched to sound and is used to check all aspects of how the film looks.

DoP – Director of Photography.

Gaffer – the chief electrician on a film set who reports to the Director of Photography. The Gaffer and his team are responsible for anything to do with the lighting, from the supply, operation and maintenance of the equipment to knowing which colour filters and gels to use.

Genre – a class or category of films that share similar characteristics in setting, plot, characters and filming techniques, for instance, Film Noir, the Western.

Grain – the uneven microscopic appearance of processed film, the development process of which can be modified to create different densities of grain.

Grip – a stagehand who carries out a range of duties from transporting and setting up equipment and scenery to pushing the wheeled platform on which the camera sits. As per the name, the Grip must have a firm grip on all equipment he or she handles.

Mis-en-scène – French term that literally means putting into the scene and refers to the way the designer has arranged all visual components to set the scene.

Narrative – the story itself.

Promo – any activity used to promote a film to generate public interest. This can range from on-set, behind-the-scenes featurettes and trailers, to advertising campaigns and press interviews.

Rushes – see Dailies.

Shoot – also known as the film shoot, it refers to the part of the process that deals with the actual shooting of the film; the photographing of a subject using a film camera.

Shot – a single, uninterrupted visual captured on camera.

Sound stage – a studio specifically designed and soundproofed for shooting a film to achieve the best results when recording dialogue.

Stock test – when colours, texture and form are tested in front of the camera with different types of film.

Strobing – where the image of a subject has a jerky, flickery effect.

Swing gang – also known as set dressers, they are responsible for getting the set ready with scenery and props needed for that day's filming and who then put away the set (known as striking the set) when it is no longer needed.

Tracking – a type of shot where the camera, usually on a wheeled platform, is moving during the shot.

Treatment – in the writing stage, this is a detailed summary of the story, ranging from ten to forty pages. It comes after the outline and before the first draft of the actual screenplay.

Wild wall – also known as a floating wall, this is a part of the set that can be moved to allow for the placement of a camera.

Bibliography

Adler, D., (ed), *Metric Handbook: Planning and Design* (Architectural Press (Elsevier), 1999)

Affron, C. and M. J., *Sets in Motion: Art Direction and Film Narrative* (Rutgers University Press, 1995)

Barnwell, J., *Production Design: Architects of the Screen* (Wallflower Press, 2004)

Belloli, A. P.A.,(mss ed) *Film Architecture: From Metropolis to Blade Runner*, (Prestel-Verlag, 1996)

Birtwistle, S., and Conklin, S., *The Making of Pride and Prejudice* (Penguin Books/BBC Books 1995)

Calloway, S., (gen ed), *The Elements of Style: An encyclopedia of domestic architectural detail* (Octopus Publishing, 1996)

Christie, I., *The Art of Film: John Box and Production Design* (Wallflower Press, 2009)

Cleland, T. M., *A Practical description of the Munsell Color System and suggestions for its use* 1937 (Kessinger Publishing, 2010)

Ede, L. N., *British Film Design: A history* (I.B. Tauris, 2010)

Ettedgui, P., *Screencraft: Cinematography* (RotoVision, 1998)

Ettedgui, P., *Screencraft: Production Design & Art Direction* (RotoVision, 1999)

Ferenczi, A., *Masters of Cinema: Tim Burton* (Cahiers du Cinema Sarl, Revised edition, 2010)

Frayling, C., *Ken Adam and The Art of Production Design* (Faber and Faber, 2005)

Hong Kong Film Arts Association (compiler), *Wild Blooms of Imagination: Art Direction in Hong Kong Films 1979–2001* (Joint Publishing (HK) Co., Ltd, 2005)

Konigsberg, I., *The Complete Film Dictionary*, Second Edition (Bloomsbury Publishing, 1997)

LoBrutto, V., *By Design: Interviews with Film Production Designers* (Praeger Publishers, 1992)

Lo Brutto, V., *The Filmmaker's Guide to Production Design* (Allworth Press, 2002)

Lord, P., and Silbey, B., *Cracking Animation: The Aardman Book of 3-D Animation* (Thames & Hudson, 1998)

Olsen, R. L., *Art Direction for Film and Video* (Focal Press, 1999)

Orton, K., *Model Making for the Stage: A Practical Guide* (The Crowood Press, 2004)

Pastoureau, M., *Blue: The History of a Color* (Princeton University Press, 2001)

Pym, J., *Time Out Film Guide* (Time Out Guides Limited, 2011)

Quintana, À., *Federico Fellini: Masters of Cinema* (Cahiers du Cinéma Sarl, Revised edition, 2011)

Salisbury, M., *Alice in Wonderland: A visual companion* (Disney Enterprises, Disney Editions, 2010)

Tangaz, T., *The Interior design course: principles, practices and techniques for the aspiring designer* (Thames & Hudson, 2006)

Tashiro, C.S., *Pretty Pictures: Production Design and the History of Film* (University of Texas Press, 1998)

Thorne, G., *Technical Drawing for Stage Design* (The Crowood Press, 2009)

Whitlock, C. and The Art Directors Guild, *Designs on Film: A Century of Hollywood Art Direction* (It Books/Harper Collins Publishing, 2010)

Recommended Viewing

FILMS

Alice In Wonderland, Director: Tim Burton (2010)

Alien, Director: Ridley Scott (1979)

Aliens, Director: James Cameron (1986)

Alien3, Director: David Fincher (1992)

Alien: Resurrection, Director: Jean-Pierre Jeunet (1997)

All About My Mother (Todo Sobre Mi Madre), Director: Pedro Almodóvar (1999)

All the President's Men, Director: Alan J. Pakula (1976)

Almost Famous, Director: Cameron Crowe (2000)

Amélie, Director: Jean-Pierre Jeunet (2001)

American Beauty, Director: Sam Mendes (1999)

An Education, Director: Lone Scherfig (2009)

Annie Hall, Director: Woody Allen (1977)

Another Year, Director: Mike Leigh (2010)

Atonement, Director: Joe Wright (2007)

Audition, Director: Takashi Miike (1999)

Australia, Director: Baz Luhrmann (2008)

Avatar, Director: James Cameron (2009)

Barry Lyndon, Director: Stanley Kubrick (1975)

Batman Begins, Director: Christopher Nolan (2005)

Beetlejuice, Director: Tim Burton (1988)

Being There, Director: Hal Ashby (1979)

Big Lebowski, The, Director: Joel Coen, Ethan Coen (Uncredited) (1998)

Big Night, Director: Campbell Scott, Stanley Tucci (1996)

Birdcage, The, Director: Mike Nichols (1996)

Birds, The, Director: Alfred Hitchcock (1963)

Black Swan, Director: Darren Aronofsky (2010)

Blade Runner, Director: Ridley Scott (1982)

Blue Velvet, Director: David Lynch (1986)

Bourne Identity, The, Director: Doug Liman (2002)

Brazil, Director: Terry Gilliam (1985)

Brighton Rock, Director: Rowan Joffe (2010)

Brokeback Mountain, Director: Ang Lee (2005)

Cabinet of Dr Caligari, The (Das Cabinet Des Dr Caligari), Director: Robert Wiene (1920)

Carla's Song, Director: Ken Loach (1996)

Casino Royale, Director: Martin Campbell (2006)

Charlie and the Chocolate Factory, Director: Tim Burton (2005)

Chinatown, Director: Roman Polanski (1974)

Chocolat, Director: Lasse Hallström (2000)

Cook, the Thief, His Wife, and Her Lover, The, Director: Peter Greenaway (1989)

Counterfeiters, The (Die Fälscher), Director: Stefan Ruzowitzky (2007)

Crouching Tiger, Hidden Dragon, Director: Ang Lee (2000)

Damned United, The, Director: Tom Hooper (2009)

Darjeeling Limited, The, Director: Wes Anderson (2007)

Dark City, Director: Alex Proyas (1998)

Dark Knight, The, Director: Christopher Nolan (2008)

Dark Water (Honogurai Mizu No Soko Kara) Director: Hideo Nakata (2002)

Das Boot, Director: Wolfgang Petersen (1981)

Derailed, Director: Mikael Håfström (2005)

Deconstructing Harry, Director: Woody Allen (1997)

Delicatessen, Director: Marc Caro, Jean-Pierre Jeunet (1991)

Desire, Director: Drew Pautz (2010)

District 9, Director: Neill Blomkamp (2009)

Dogville, Director: Lars von Trier (2003)

Don't Look Now, Director: Nicolas Roeg (1973)

Doubt, Director: John Patrick Shanley (2008)

Down with Love, Director: Peyton Reed (2003)

Downfall (Der Untergang), Director: Oliver Hirschbiegel (2004)

Dr No, Director: Terence Young (1962)

Ed Wood, Director: Tim Burton (1994)

Edward Scissorhands, Director: Tim Burton (1990)

Elephant Man, The, Director: David Lynch (1980)

Fallen Angels (Duo Luo Tian Shi), Director: Kar Wai Wong (1995)

Fantastic Mr Fox, Director: Wes Anderson (2009)

Fargo, Director: Joel Coen and Ethan Coen (Uncredited) (1996)

Fellini's Casanova (Il Casanova di Federico Fellini), Director: Federico Fellini (1976)

Fifth Element, The, Director: Luc Besson (1997)

Fight Club, Director: David Fincher (1999)

Frida, Director: Julie Taymor (2002)

From Russia With Love, Director: Terence Young (1963)

Gattaca, Director: Andrew Niccol (1997)

Girl With a Pearl Earring, Director: Peter Webber (2003)

Godfather, The, Director: Francis Ford Coppola (1972)

Godfather, The: Part II, Director: Francis Ford Coppola (1974)

GoldenEye, Director: Martin Campbell (1995)

Goldfinger, Director: Guy Hamilton (1964)

Goodbye Lenin!, Director: Wolfgang Becker (2003)

Good Night, and Good Luck, Director: George Clooney (2005)

Gosford Park, Director: Robert Altman (2001)

Grudge, The (Ju-on), Director: Takashi Shimizu (2002)

Harold and Maude, Director: Hal Ashby (1971)

Harry Potter and the Philosopher's Stone, Director: Chris Columbus (2001)

Harry Potter and the Chamber of Secrets, Director: Chris Columbus (2002)

Harry Potter and the Prisoner of Azkaban, Director: Alfonso Cuaron (2004)

Harry Potter and the Goblet of Fire, Director: Mike Newell (2005)

Harry Potter and the Order of the Phoenix, Director: David Yates (2007)

Harry Potter and the Half-Blood Prince, Director: David Yates (2009)

Harry Potter and the Deathly Hallows: Part 1, Director: David Yates (2010)

Harry Potter and the Deathly Hallows: Part 2, Director: David Yates (2011)

Hero (Ying Xiong), Director: Yimou Zhang (2002)

Hidden (Caché), Director: Michael Haneke (2005)

How to Marry a Millionaire, Director: Jean Negulesco (1953)

Howards End, Director: James Ivory (1992)

Hurt Locker, The, Director: Kathryn Bigelow (2008)

I Am Love (Io Sono L'Amore), Director: Luca Guadagnino (2009)

I've Loved You So Long (Il y a longtemps que je t'aime), Director: Philippe Claudel (2008)

Inland Empire, Director: David Lynch (2006)

Iron Man, Director: Jon Favreau (2008)

Jane Eyre, Director: Cary Fukunaga (2011)

Julie & Julia, Director: Nora Ephron (2009)

Kes, Director: Ken Loach (1969)

Kill Bill: Vol. 1, Director: Quentin Tarantino (2003)

Kill Bill: Vol. 2, Director: Quentin Tarantino (2004)

King's Speech, The, Director: Tom Hooper (2010)

La Dolce Vita, Director: Federico Fellini (1960)

La Jetée, Director: Chris Marker (1962)

Léon, Director: Luc Besson (1994)

Let the Right One In (Låt Den Rätte Komma In), Director: Tomas Alfredson (2008)

Lives of Others, The (Das Leben der Anderen), Director: Florian Henckel von Donnersmarck (2006)

Lock, Stock and Two Smoking Barrels, Director: Guy Ritchie (1998)

Lord of the Rings, The: The Fellowship of the Ring, Director: Peter Jackson (2001)

Lord of the Rings, The: The Two Towers, Director: Peter Jackson (2002)

Lord of the Rings, The: The Return of the King, Director: Peter Jackson (2003)

Lost Highway, Director: David Lynch (1997)

Lost in La Mancha, Director: Keith Fulton, Louis Pepe (2002)

Lost In Translation, Director: Sofia Coppola (2003)

Mad Max, Director: George Miller (1979)

Mad Max Beyond Thunderdome, Director: George Miller, George Ogilvie (1985)

Madness of King George, The, Director: Nicholas Hytner (1994)

Man In The White Suit, The, Director: Alexander Mackendrick (1951)

Manhattan, Director: Woody Allen (1979)

Matrix, The, Director: Andy Wachowski, Lana Wachowski (1999)

Memento, Director: Christopher Nolan (2000)

Metropolis, Director: Fritz Lang (1927)

Micmacs (Micmacs à tire-larigot), Director: Jean-Pierre Jeunet (2009)

Misery, Director: Rob Reiner (1990)

Mon Oncle, Director: Jacques Tati (1958)

Monsoon Wedding, Director: Mira Nair (2001)

Moon, Director: Duncan Jones (2009)

Morvern Callar, Director: Lynne Ramsay (2002)

Moulin Rouge!, Director: Baz Luhrmann (2001)

Mulholland Drive, Director: David Lynch (2001)

Mystery Train, Director: Jim Jarmusch (1989)

Never Let Me Go, Director: Mark Romanek (2010)

Niagara, Director: Henry Hathaway (1953)

Nil By Mouth, Director: Gary Oldman (1997)

No Country for Old Men, Director: Ethan Coen, Joel Coen (2007)

Nosferatu (Nosferatu, eine Symphonie des Grauens), Director: F.W. Murnau (1922)

Notting Hill, Director: Roger Michell (1999)

Omen, The, Director: Richard Donner (1976)

One Hour Photo, Director: Mark Romanek (2002)

Orlando, Director: Sally Potter (1992)

Orphanage, The (El Orfanato), Director: Juan Antonio Bayona (2007)

Oscar and Lucinda, Director: Gillian Armstrong (1997)

Our Man In Havana, Director: Carol Reed (1959)

Out of Sight, Director: Steven Soderbergh (1998)

Pan's Labyrinth (El Laberinto del Fauno), Director: Guillermo del Toro (2006)

Paranormal Activity, Director: Oren Peli (2007)

Paris, Je T'Aime, Director: Various (2006)

Pillow Book, The, Director: Peter Greenaway (1996)

Pillow Talk, Director: Michael Gordon (1959)

Play Time, Director: Jacques Tati (1967)

Prêt-à-Porter, Director: Robert Altman (1994)

Prophet, A (Un Prophète), Director: Jacques Audiard (2009)

Psycho, Director: Alfred Hitchcock (1960)

Raging Bull, Director: Martin Scorsese (1980)

Indiana Jones and the Raiders of the Lost Ark, Director: Steven Spielberg (1981)

Raining Stones, Director: Ken Loach (1993)

Read My Lips (Sur Mes Lèvres), Director: Jacques Audiard (2001)

Reader, The, Director: Stephen Daldry (2008)

Rear Window, Director: Alfred Hitchcock (1954)

Remains of the Day, The, Director: James Ivory (1993)

Reservoir Dogs, Director: Quentin Tarantino (1992)

Revolutionary Road, Director: Sam Mendes (2008)

Ring (Ringu), Director: Hideo Nakata (1998)

Room With A View, A, Director: James Ivory (1985)

Rope, Director: Alfred Hitchcock (1948)

Run Lola Run (Lola rennt), Director: Tom Tykwer (1998)

Sans Soleil, Director: Chris Marker (1983)

Saturday Night Fever, Director: John Badham (1977)

Secretary, Director: Steven Shainberg (2002)

Sense and Sensibility, Director: Ang Lee (1995)

Shadow of the Vampire, Director: E. Elias Merhige (2000)

Romeo and Juliet, Director: Baz Luhrmann (1996)

Shining, The, Director: Stanley Kubrick (1980)

Short Cuts, Director: Robert Altman (1993)

Shutter Island, Director: Martin Scorsese (2010)

Sideways, Director: Alexander Payne (2004)

Silence of The Lambs, The, Director: Jonathan Demme (1991)

Silk Stockings, Director: Rouben Mamoulian (1957)

Sin City, Director: Frank Miller, Robert Rodriguez, Quentin Tarantino (2005)

Single Man, A, Director: Tom Ford (2009)

Skin I Live In, The (La piel que habito), Director: Pedro Almodóvar (2011)

Sleepy Hollow, Director: Tim Burton (1999)

Slumdog Millionaire, Director: Danny Boyle, Loveleen Tandan (2008)

Snatch, Director: Guy Ritchie (2000)

Solaris, Director: Steven Soderbergh (2002)

Some Like It Hot, Director: Billy Wilder (1959)

Star Wars: Episode I (The Phantom Menace), Director: George Lucas (1999)

Star Wars: Episode II (Attack of the Clones), Director: George Lucas (2002)

Star Wars: Episode III (Revenge of the Sith), Director: George Lucas (2005)

Star Wars: Episode IV (A New Hope), Director: George Lucas (1977)

Star Wars: Episode V (The Empire Strikes Back), Director: Irvin Kershner (1980)

Star Wars: Episode VI (Return of the Jedi), Director: Richard Marquand (1983)

Strictly Ballroom, Director: Baz Luhrmann (1992)

Submarine, Director: Richard Ayoade (2010)

Syriana, Director: Stephen Gaghan (2005)

Tempest, The, Director: Julie Taymor (2010)

Thin Red Line, The, Director: Terrence Malick (1998)

This Is England, Director: Shane Meadows (2006)

Tinker Tailor Soldier Spy, Director: Tomas Alfredson (2011)

Topsy-Turvy, Director: Mike Leigh (1999)

Traffic, Director: Steven Soderbergh (2000)

Trainspotting, Director: Danny Boyle (1996)
Twelve Monkeys, Director: Terry Gilliam (1995)
Vanity Fair, Director: Mira Nair (2004)
Vera Drake, Director: Mike Leigh (2004)
Vertigo, Director: Alfred Hitchcock (1958)
Volver, Director: Pedro Almodóvar (2006)
Wait Until Dark, Director: Terence Young (1967)
We Need To Talk About Kevin, Director: Lynne Ramsay (2011)
Wedding Banquet, The (Xi Yan), Director: Ang Lee (1993)
What Ever Happened to Baby Jane?, Director: Robert Aldrich (1962)
Wonderland, Director: Michael Winterbottom (1999)
X-Men, Director: Bryan Singer (2000)
You've Got Mail, Director: Nora Ephron (1998)

TELEVISION

Ashes to Ashes, Yr 1, Director: Various (2008)
Ashes to Ashes, Yr 2 , Director: Various (2009)
Ashes to Ashes, Yr 3, Director: Various (2010)
Bleak House, Director: Justin Chadwick, Susanna White (2005)
Carnivàle, Yr 1, Director: Various (2003)
Carnivàle, Yr 2, Director: Various (2005)
Cranford, Yr 1, Director: Simon Curtis, Steve Hudson (2007)
Cranford, Yr 2, Director: Simon Curtis, Steve Hudson (2009)
Deadwood, Yr 1, Director: Various (2004)
Deadwood, Yr 2, Director: Various (2005)
Deadwood, Yr 3, Director: Various (2006)
Downton Abbey, Yr 1, Director: Various (2010)
Downton Abbey, Yr 2, Director: Various (2011)
Hour, The, Director: Harry Bradbeer, Coky Giedroyc, Jamie Payne (2011)
League of Gentlemen, The, Yr 1, Director: Steve Bendelack (1999)
League of Gentlemen, The, Yr 2, Director: Steve Bendelack (2000)
League of Gentlemen, The, Yr 3, Director: Steve Bendelack (2002)

Life on Mars, Yr 1, Director: Various (2006)
Life on Mars, Yr 2, Director: Various (2007)
Lost, Yr 1, Director: Various (2004)
Lost, Yr 2, Director: Various (2005)
Lost, Yr 3, Director: Various (2006)
Lost, Yr 4, Director: Various (2008)
Lost, Yr 5, Director: Various (2009)
Lost, Yr 6, Director: Various (2010)
Mad Men, Yr 1, Director: Various (2007)
Mad Men, Yr 2, Director: Various (2008)
Mad Men, Yr 3, Director: Various (2009)
Mad Men, Yr 4, Director: Various (2010)
Mad Men, Yr 5, Director: Various (2012)
Mildred Pierce, Director: Todd Haynes (2011)
Pride and Prejudice, Director: Simon Langton (1995)
Psychoville, Yr 1, Director: Matt Lipsey (2009)
Psychoville, Yr 2, Director: Matt Lipsey (2010)
Shadow Line, The, Director: Hugo Blick (2011)
This Is England '86, Director: Tom Harper, Shane Meadows (2010)
Twin Peaks, Yr 1, Director: David Lynch, *et al.* (1990)
Twin Peaks, Yr 2, Director: David Lynch, *et al.* (1991)
Upstairs, Downstairs, Director: Euros Lyn (2010)
Wire, The, Yr 1, Director: Various (2002)
Wire, The, Yr 2, Director: Various (2003)
Wire, The, Yr 3, Director: Various (2004)
Wire, The, Yr 4, Director: Various (2006)
Wire, The, Yr 5, Director: Various (2008)
X-Files, The, Yr 1, Director: Various (1993)
X-Files, The, Yr 2, Director: Various (1994)
X-Files, The, Yr 3, Director: Various (1995)
X-Files, The, Yr 4, Director: Various (1996)
X-Files, The, Yr 5, Director: Various (1997)
X-Files, The, Yr 6, Director: Various (1998)
X-Files, The, Yr 7, Director: Various (1999)
X-Files, The, Yr 8, Director: Various (2000)
X-Files, The, Yr 9, Director: Various (2001)
Red Riding: In the Year of Our Lord 1974, Director: Julian Jarrold (2009)
Red Riding: In the Year of Our Lord 1980, Director: James Marsh (2009)
Red Riding: In the Year of Our Lord 1983, Director: Anand Tucker (2009)

INDEX